—THE— ACCIDENTAL EDUCATOR

—THE—
ACCIDENTAL EDUCATOR

Life-Defining Stories of Rites and Wrongs

Dr. Eric Reno

gatekeeper press™

Tampa, Florida

The Accidental Educator: Life-Defining Stories of Rites and Wrongs

Published by Gatekeeper Press
7853 Gunn Hwy, Suite 209
Tampa, FL 33626
www.GatekeeperPress.com

Cover Design: Jenny Fischer, *Fischer Creative*

Library of Congress Control Number: 2023931408

ISBN (hardcover): 9781662932236
ISBN (paperback): 9781662932243
eISBN: 9781662932250

Student Testimonials

"Eric: Please see the comments students have written about your presentations. Clearly you continue to make an impact. Thank you so much again for offering your wisdom and time. While this is meant to bless the students, listening to your lectures is always so inspiring for me as well. I always leave learning something new."

Dr. Christina Minihan,
Professor of Tourism & Journalism
Colorado State University
Best Teacher of the Year, 2022:
CSU Alumni Association

"One of my key takeaways was the sense of... almost wonder? that Reno has about life. It is whimsical and a very positive outlook that I believe is important to live by. Many of his key points are almost cliches, but they are so prevalent for a reason."

"I really valued his thoughts and will cherish Dr. Reno's letter for the rest of my life. Thank you for including this in the course."

"One thing Dr. Reno preaches is to choose your friends wisely, and if your current friends are not fulfilling you the way a friendship should, 'cut them loose."

"My biggest takeaway from this amazing interview was to just not underestimate yourself. I loved this interview. Thank you so much for this professor!"

"I liked what Dr. Reno said about enjoying people who offer things we don't excel in. We often focus on ourselves and what we bring to the table, and forget that others can make us better and stronger and smarter."

"My favorite self-reflection piece was definitely by Dr. Reno. People like Dr. Reno make me believe there are still good, wholesome people in the world that want to see young people succeed."

"I love Dr. Reno's point, 'Don't let others tell you who you are. That is your responsibility."

"My favorite takeaway from Dr. Reno was his last point which states: 'Everyone has opinions. Listen only to those who can back them up.' I'm so thankful for this lesson, especially right now, and I needed to hear this!"

"One key thing he said was that 'We are all walking resumes' and that made me think about how people view me. I am disabled and have spent most of my life ashamed of it, only to grow to love my disabled identity in college and discover my dream for being an advocate and role model. Reno's comments made me realize that since being disabled is my brand, why am I not showing the full, raw experiences of it instead of manicuring a good perfect image of a disabled person?"

"Dr. Reno had so many wise words but the takeaway that I want to apply to my own self-growth is: 'Never underestimate your ability to positively impact the lives of others by actions you take and behaviors you exhibit.' My self-growth is becoming the best version of myself for my daughter."

"One key takeaway from Dr. Reno's presentation and letter was to never stop being curious and to watch, listen and read critically. What he says about growing outside the boarders of our own senses is so important."

"The person we were growing up is not necessarily the person we will become.' This was the main takeaway I got from Dr. Reno."

"My favorite content is from Dr. Reno. This is a conversation I didn't expect. I thought I would go to class as usual, but after turning to him I wondered if I was too shy to face myself, too afraid to give up before trying."

"My favorite content came from Dr. Reno. I've never experienced such emotion integrated into teaching. It came as a surprise and gave me an inside look into the true depth behind the course – the 'why' behind it."

"I loved the lecture from Dr. Reno. It was a casual conversation that felt like talking to one of my grandparents about life and how to live. The letter of tips was amazing."

"I loved our conversation with Dr. Reno and his letter to us. It made my day to hear him talk about his life. His words made an impact on me as a graduating senior, and I'm thankful for the time we spent with him."

"I have never experienced this type of positive self-reflection in a class. If I had to choose one, I think I would go with the lecture and tips from Dr. Reno."

Dedication

This work is dedicated to my immediate family who are my life and to my extended generational family who have provided a solid foundation. Those of additional influence and support are referenced throughout the memoir.

Contents

Introduction

On a mid-month March Friday in 2013, I sent out a broadcast email announcing my decision to retire at the end of the calendar year after ten rewarding years as the founding president of Northeast Lakeview College, the newest of the five colleges in the Alamo Community College District, serving the greater San Antonio area. The following Monday I received a call from my doctor informing me I had tested positive for prostate cancer, a stark reminder that lives end, and not always at the most opportune time.

I had never faced serious health issues and mortality was always in the distant future, and the domain of others. A year later I was on the table for eight hours of open-heart surgery. I received wonderful medical treatment and resumed an active and rewarding retirement of golfing, consulting, and grandfathering. But my life had changed, and the perspective of my future with it. What was important, and what needed my immediate attention?

For years I have wanted to write something of value, but that vague goal was missing form and content. A further assessment of my literary intent was the obvious realization we have one life. That's all we get, not counting the hereafter. I was at that stage where memories outpaced dreams, where life is measured in quarter centuries, and where the circle of friends gets smaller each year. But I marvel at my good fortune to have observed and participated in the historical, political, cultural, social, and technological changes that have spanned almost a century.

On occasions I mounted my soapbox and became a regular in the letter-to-the-editor pages of local newspapers, acquiring a loyal following of supporters and angry opposers. My role in building a new community college and a new culture was a section cover page of the April 28, 2006, edition of the national higher education publication, *The Chronicle of Higher Education*. A full back-cover article on teaching excellence was published June 3, 2011. The national political environment of the 2016 presidential election became the topic of angry letters, essays, and emails. My efforts were limited. I was one of thousands voicing the sound and fury that demanded logic and a crusade against ignorance. We were voices in the wilderness. My motivation to produce a volume of value beyond brief and limited issues was gaining urgency.

Publishers ask the genre of submitted manuscripts. I had the choice of memoir or autobiography. I concluded that autobiography was a chronological story of a person – the people, places, and events of a life. My understanding of a memoir is that it is the same story, with overlays of reflection and greater freedom in the manipulation of time and place.

Writing about a life doesn't make it any more special than others, but hopefully reveals and offers occasional thought-provoking observations. The voice of Socrates prompted me to examine the unexamined and isolate the junctures that give purpose to that wellspring that began as formless energy. The goal was to write, not just about a life, but also of a time. It was time to put on the tin hat, turn on the frontal lamp, descend into the shaft of dimming memory, and begin mining for meaning – not sure where I was headed or what I would find.

I recalled moments that might provide a worthwhile telling. I was purposely invisible in high school: never chosen, recognized, nor involved. I was not considered college material and began my post-high school career breaking concrete blocks and sweeping up the debris. A year and a half later I was an Air Force intelligence analyst, with a *Top Secret Codeword* clearance, based in the United Kingdom, reporting regularly to the National Security Agency (NSA), and recruited as a civilian employee upon discharge from the service after my four-year enlistment.

But I was determined to become my family's first college graduate. I succeeded and spent five years in the corporate culture, finally deciding it wasn't a fit. My next goal was to teach English at the college level, though never having been at the front of a classroom. At age thirty I began the pursuit of my dream, with no job, experience, prospects, money, but with a supportive wife and our first child on the way. Forty years later I retired as a college president.

This memoir is about the journey: the events, decisions, lessons, places, and people who played roles in shaping a life that could never have been envisioned those many years ago.

ESSAYS to MYSELF

Included within this memoir are selected essays written over the years that have served as anger outlets and calming correspondence. I have included those that seem to fit – providing immediacy, distance, and perspective to complement topics being remembered.

Prologue

The Mississippi River begins somewhere. To be precise, in Lake Itasca, Minnesota. Its path carves varied formations – gaining strength and establishing and changing history. But it does end, discharging jetsam and flotsam along the way. Folk wisdom states that life is like a river. We spring from a common source and empty into that great body called a life. The flow is interrupted by changing currents and depths, dams and diversions. How do we cause or react to the intermittent barriers? Do we merge, grow, or turn into a trickle?

2,365,200,000	Seconds
39,420,000	Minutes
657,000	Hours
27,376	Days
3,900	Weeks
900	Months
75	Years

Some things must begin at the end if one is to attach any significance to the beginning. Assuming an average lifespan of seventy-five years, the numbers above reflect our allotment for growth and maturity, success and failure, celebration and tragedy, ecstasy and depression, and the intervening forces of fate, luck, karma, predestination, Divine intervention, and choice. This time can be seen as the greatest gift, a trial to be cursed, or just something to be endured.

1. The RITES of LIFE

A rite of passage is a door into a room we never knew existed, leaving behind a room we will never occupy again. Rites are universal and unique to individual circumstances. My look back involves the rites that have directed my life, for good or bad. They color and flavor and at times, poison. They are uniquely mine.

The chapters of this journey intersect, overlap, and connect. The events are not linear nor are they chronological. They do not stand alone. References reflect their place, their effect on my perceptions, and the roles played in my personal growth and development. I view the rites in how I experience the works of French Impressionists. I stand in front of a painting, nose to canvas, and am dazzled by the pattern of gloriously colored dots. As I retreat I see shapes and shadows, and then the final vision of the artist, its beauty increasing as I change distances and angles, generating different emotions, seeing multiple stories as I move.

My references to prominent figures do not necessarily reflect commonly held assessments of their stature and place in history. I used Ernest Hemingway as a generational touchstone and an introductory guide. He spoke to me because he lived a life I dreamed of.

In the mid 20th Century, for many impressionable young males, Hemingway stood as the model of what it meant to be a man. I could surely learn from him what I needed to accomplish to enter manhood. But it was the adventurer, not the writer, that I wanted to emulate. He traveled the world, hunted big game, fought wars, proved irresistible to beautiful women, and wrote some of the most popular novels and affecting short stories in the English language.

Then I discovered the divide between the public perception and the artist's work. The work was where I would learn, but Hemingway's stories initially told me nothing.

I realized I had to pay attention to every detail on the page. As I grew into his stories I discovered there was no closure, only experiences that forced questions and ultimately provided answers. Critics reference the "code" in Hemingway's stories that reinforces a man's responsibility for his own behavior, his own values, his own character. There is no one else to credit or blame. The phrase "grace under pressure" is also a referenced behavior, something that a man should aspire to, but a behavior that can never be predicted until it is tested.

His short stories have Nick Adams as the main character in almost a third. Each story stands on its own as a rite, from childhood to old age, that will change how Nick and other main characters perceive the world, influencing and fashioning the person they will become. I am attempting to isolate my elements, those dabs of color and those seemingly standalone events, to see how they have contributed to shaping a life approaching its end.

When I taught I used Hemingway's short stories to discuss literature as the marriage of form and content. The short story, "Hills Like White Elephants," does what Hemingway does best, providing clues to tell a story. It's up to the reader to find the depth that will reveal its substance. The story does not involve Nick Adams but does offer a young couple who are obviously in love, and based on destination labels on their luggage, having a wonderful time traveling Europe. We meet them at the station bar sipping drinks and waiting for their connecting train. The countryside is dry and barren on one side of the tracks and green and lush on the other. Their first bit of conversation lets us know there is an issue being avoided. The couple dance around the topic, but the dialogue reveals, by tone and content, that it needs to be addressed.

When I ask students what is going on I get observations about their relationship and their travel. I ask if there is any significance in the surrounding countryside, explaining that good writers, especially in short stories, include only details contributing to the meaning of the story. At this point I share a story Harry Crews told his sophomore-level creative writing course at Broward Junior College in 1965 concerning advice from the Russian writer, Anton Chekov, who stated that a gun hanging on the wall at the beginning of a story had better have discharged by the end.

The students soon grasp the tension between the couple, and someone raises a hand and states: "They are discussing whether or not to have an abortion." The students are now paying attention and asking how their colleague came to that conclusion. The more they talk the more they agree that is the issue. This four-page story then comes to life, and they start seeing significance in snatches of dialogue, adding tone to words and sentences, seeing importance in the setting and what it contributes to the story. The difference in the characters' attitudes toward the abortion and how it will affect the life they have become accustomed to is now the focus of the discussion. The man is in favor of abortion because a child will change their ability to do what and when they want, and the woman's less obvious stance proposes a child might deepen their relationship.

I ask if everyone knows the meaning of the phrase "white elephant"? Some have been to a white elephant party where gifts that no one wants are passed on. I share that my wife and I were gifted a clock mounted on a beautifully finished piece of wood. The craftmanship was obvious. The only problem was that the wood had a large and highly glossed picture of an orangutang. No telling how many parties it has graced over the decades. But the point has been made. The four-word title summarizes the dilemma.

I then ask if the couple will get an abortion and, if so, what is the future of the relationship? Opinions are varied and passionate. I then ask: "Is this what the story is about?" They wonder what else it could be about. I then ask: "Have you ever loved, idolized, or admired someone so much they could do nothing wrong in your eyes, but in an instant they did something that forever changed your feelings about them?"

Every class has the same reaction. Discussions cease and minds identify the person and the event. Heads begin to shake, and though I never ask anyone to share who or what, many volunteer, making the point of the story more dramatic and emotional than I ever could. Even if the male character agrees to the abortion, will their relationship ever be the same? Will it survive that universal rite of disappointment and tragic awareness that comes in everyone's life as they mature and encounter new experiences? Their perception of literature has changed. It has become personal.

Other Hemingway stories provide teaching opportunities that open students' minds to the practicality of literature, and its reflection of their individual lives. "Indian Camp" finds a very young Nick encountering an unexpected and tragic event far beyond his developmental ability to understand and his father's ability to explain. Nick is left having to use his limited life experience to make sense of the incomprehensible, deciding the event was something that happened to other and older people.

In the story, "The Killers," we encounter Nick as a young man bumming around the country and working in a rural diner. Two men enter, dressed in dark suits out of place for the rural community and worn in a fashion that says they are not businessmen. They sit at the counter and ask if this is where the Swede works and, if so, when does he come to work? They are told the Swede doesn't come to work for some time. They say they will wait and when asked why they wanted to see him, they calmly state they are going to kill him.

The Swede doesn't show up and the men leave. Nick announces he should tell the Swede about the men and runs from the diner intent on saving his life. He finds him in his room, lying in bed, in the dark. Nick breathlessly tells all that happened and that if the Swede leaves immediately he can escape the two men. The Swede thanks Nick but doesn't move. Nick races back to the diner, tells his co-workers what happened, and says it's too awful and he must leave. End of story, which leaves students wondering what the story was about. We discuss events in our lives that we didn't understand and could not explain. They are rites that change how we look at the world. We know there is a story behind the Swede's acceptance of his fate, but there is nothing that helps us to understand. The world becomes more frightening and complex as Nick's innocence is diminished.

"A Clean, Well-Lighted Place" is a story about the end of life. Choices lessen, your importance is of less value to others, and happiness, or contentment, require fewer material trappings. Something as simple as a clean, well-lighted place is all you seek.

My favorite Hemingway short story is, "Big Two-Hearted River." The only character is Nick Adams. He is seeking a place that will provide safety and help heal from an event never explained. That place is the woods of Northern Michigan where he frequently went fishing with friends. Was the damage physical or psychological? How old is Nick? How long ago were the times he remembers? How long since he was last there? No details given. He is precise in following every movement and action he remembers, knowing how crucial it is to be true to his memories if he is to heal.

Students usually react to the story in a similar manner. There are looks of disbelief that this is my favorite story. They question my love for a story about someone going fishing. I ask leading questions and remind them every detail is significant. The story begins to expand, their questions and perceptions gain depth. They begin to understand why the scenes of Nick looking into the stream to see fish fighting to hold themselves steady in the current and discovering that a burned-out portion of the woods has grasshoppers that have been burned black, but are still alive.

They begin to understand why Nick cannot take a shortcut, but must follow the trail always taken and why the excitement of catching his first fish is too much for him, and he is forced to sit down. We eventually shift from Nick's refuge of safety to each of us. I ask if they have a site, or remembrance, physical or emotional, where they seek comfort during times of stress or loss? Most are eager to share their private retreat, giving reasons for its origin and stories of its importance in their lives.

At the end of our discussion I share an excerpt from another short story featuring Nick Adams, "Now I Lay Me." Nick is in a hospital recovering from a serious war wound and believes if he falls asleep, he will die. To stay awake he remembers fishing trips he took regularly with his friends. This memory would keep him alive. Both stories stand alone, but each provides a satisfying complement to the other.

* * *

My "Big Two-Hearted River" was baseball. In my youth it was my retreat, my haven. I loved the history and traditions, the personalities, the math, the myths, the physics, and the symmetry. I loved the drama and the variety of skills required to be successful. I liked the solitary roles and the unity of teamwork. Tuesday was the most important day of the week – when the latest edition of the weekly baseball bible, *The Sporting News*, would arrive at our local drug store. I read every word about every team, hoping my Kansas City Athletics might be developing players capable of raising the team out of its annual last place finish.

Baseball kept me afloat during the flood waters of adolescence, providing the potential for acceptance, accomplishment, and recognition. At age thirteen I was a solitary traveler, taking and changing buses for twenty miles each way to get to practices and games, often at night, changing buses in the dark downtown terminal, not getting home until 10:00pm, something we would never allow our children to do now.

I could not run or hit with any skill, so my efforts focused on the position of pitcher – a position vital to the team but unique in its solitary function. Every pitch was a laboratory, unconsciously determining the analytics of varying speeds, angles, and curvature. Every game provided twenty-seven mini-dramas, most involving the efforts and results of the pitcher.

I am still a fan, and there are times, well into my adult life, when I still reflect on the three or four moments where I excelled, surprising myself and all I had played with and against. The following essay revives one of those times.

1992: BRIAN PICCOLO and the ZONE

Bruce Springsteen's song "Glory Days" is the anthem of thousands of American males in their declining and reclining years as they relive the moment they sank the winning basket, got the game-winning hit, or scored the winning touchdown. Baseball spring training signals those memories for me, and the events of one special day. For a lucky few whose physical skills never matched aspirations, there is a moment when the convergence of cosmic forces – mind, body, and situation, come together as they never have before and rarely, if ever, will again. Athletes call it "being in the zone." It has happened to me twice: once for a thirty-minute stretch of a poker game while I was in the service when I knew, without looking, that I could draw one card to an inside straight, and one summer day in Ft. Lauderdale, Florida, in 1960.

I had just graduated from high school and was playing my last season of summer baseball, waiting to leave for Air Force basic training. My fantasy was to play professional baseball, but my high school career produced exactly two game appearances. And though my high school career barely registered, I was a summer league whiz. I was usually the star pitcher on the recreation department-sponsored team, composed of players not good enough to be drafted by teams with commercial sponsors. The previous year, due to a lack of funds, the city gave us Bermuda shorts instead of the traditional long pants. The only thing we led the league in was missing the steal sign.

I did very well as a right-handed pitcher, with an exaggerated over-hand motion, who threw a wide variety of pitches: a mediocre fastball, changeup, curves from every angle and at every speed, the only forkball (now called a splitter) in the county, and excellent control. Though I played on the worst team in the Summer League, I looked forward to playing the best teams – pitching against players I was not good enough to pitch against in high school. The best team in the league had a mini-murderers' row, with the best athlete in the county, Brian Piccolo, as their star. The summer was the only time I got to see Brian; I attended public school, and he attended parochial school.

Over the years we had established a nodding acquaintance. Brian was friendly to everyone and unimpressed by his own reputation On the day I was to face Brian's team I knew we didn't have a chance of winning, but I didn't want to embarrass myself in front of the largest crowd of the season, including some pro scouts – none of whom had come to see me. I was able to get two fast strikes on the first two right-handed batters, and on each occasion my catcher signaled for a side-arm fastball, hoping to get them to bail out of the batter's box. But when I threw from that unfamiliar angle, a totally unexpected thing happened: the side-arm pitch had a velocity and movement beyond anything I had ever achieved and seemed to explode ten feet from the plate, rising from the belt to the chest.

After a few more batters and many side-arm fastballs we decided to stay with that pitch completely until the batters showed they could hit it. They never did. The results were astounding, and I was astounded by what I could do: throw every pitch with the absolute certainty I was in complete control. Most of the batters had hit against me many times, and I had always been a comfortable out. No matter how often I got them out, it was always their mistake and had nothing to do with my ability. By their third at-bat most expected nothing more than their three swings. On that day I was convinced that Mickey Mantle and Willie Mays would have had trouble hitting me.

Through eight innings I had 17 strikeouts. The score was 0-0 and "Pic" was leading off the ninth. I had struck him out the first two times up and started off with two side-arm fastballs for strikes. Then, for a reason I still cannot explain, I thought how much fun it would be to throw my first changeup of the day, catching him by complete surprise. My catcher seemed bewildered when I shook off the sign for the side-arm fastball. He signaled again, and I shook him off. Finally, he went through my whole repertoire of pitches until I acknowledged the sign for the changeup curveball. He shook his head in disgust and set up for the pitch.

The second the ball left my hand I wanted to call timeout. Brian's eyes reflected no surprise and, to this day, I don't understand how he knew what was coming. He drove the ball deep to left field, above where a fence should have been, into a stand of trees. The ball ricocheted from tree to tree and fell at the feet of the left fielder. Lulled by the apparent destination of the ball, Brian did not initially run at full speed and was thrown out at the plate. He dusted himself off and turned to give me the trace of a smile. That was our last encounter. Unfortunately, they scored an unearned run in the 10th inning, but I finished with 20 strikeouts and, in the era of the bonus baby, I was sure I was next.

We know what became of Brian: star running back at Wake Forest; Chicago Bear's running mate of NFL Hall of Famer, Gayle Sayers; tragic death by cancer at an early age; and subject of one of our best-loved sports movies, *Brian's Song* (1971), remade in 2001. What became of my newfound ability? I couldn't wait until my next start to see how I would do against a team with average ability. Word had also gotten out and a few curious scouts came to see me. But the magic was gone. The side-arm fastball did nothing out of the ordinary and was difficult to control. I reverted to my kitchen sink style of pitching – good enough for service and college ball, but not the pros.

On that day, for the first time, I saw uncertainty in their eyes and, at times, fear. I do not understand the physics, physiology, luck, or karma that allowed me to perform at a level far above that which I had ever achieved before or would ever achieve afterward. But during every spring training season I luxuriate in the belief that I knew, if only for a moment, what Sandy Koufax, Bob Gibson, Nolan Ryan, and Randy Johnson felt on their best days. The only blemish on that memory is the image of delight and anticipation in Brian Piccolo's eyes – a blemish that makes the event all the more worth remembering.

Dr. Eric Reno
Broward Community College
Fort Lauderdale News-Sun Sentinel, 1992

2. The FOUNDATION

A building will collapse without it.

I am a fourth generation midwestern WASP (White Anglo Saxon Protestant) raised in a loving and extended family. I was modeled traditional values and hard work and was raised to be a good person. That was the extent of what was expected of me. I am also a life-long registered political *Independent* and was once considered a Christian.

I am from a generation and carry its genetic code and have contributed to how it will be remembered. I am a prisoner of an inherited environment, the people related and the places surrounding. The eternal debate of nature versus nurture was overshadowed by the luck of the draw as we evolved, bouncing between incidental and random forces that would refine who we were and shape who we would become.

I am an in-utero child of the Second World War (WWII), a minus-five-month veteran of Pearl Harbor. That fact, more than anything else, has shaped how I perceive the world. The horror, courage, and romance of that era formed beliefs and principles, our perspective of the past and hopes for the future, and our world view and sense of place. What we read, listened to, watched, and talked about were directly and indirectly colored by the events involving the clearly good and bad, the right and wrong, that cost fifty million lives, most of them innocent.

There was a great advantage in living when events seemed to move in real time – and at times, slow motion – contrasted to the pace of events and information we live in now. In the 1940s and 50s we learned in schoolrooms that accommodated maps we believed showed permanent names and boundaries. There were time slots for information: the morning and evening newspapers and electronic news limited to fifteen minutes per day, usually at dinnertime. We were confident that persons of note were so designated based on a meritocracy. We assumed that only the best and brightest were awarded positions of leadership and prominence.

Our families modeled adult behavior, not perfectly but consistently. We flourished in the community of our early years in Overland Park, Kansas, complemented by the homestead of extended family in Wayland, Michigan. The expectations were clear, the institutions nurturing, the family and community values shared.

Sept. 2020: GRANDMA RENO DIED TODAY

On January 31, 2020, I finished the final entry of Grandma Mae Reno's daily diaries that began in 1930 and ended six days prior to her passing in 1963. She died at home in Wayland, Michigan. Grandpa Reno completed the journal with the entry: "She was a noble wife and mother. May she rest in peace. Dad."

We first became aware of the diaries at a family reunion in 1985 when Aunt Ruth walked into our gathering room with a box and told us to enjoy the reading material. Most of us grabbed the year we were born and looked for additional personal references. Fast forward to 2019 when my wife, Pat, and I visited cousin Pete (Lee) and wife, Gina, in Washington, D.C. Pete had just finished the diaries and thought I might enjoy going beyond the year of my birth, given an additional thirty-five years of life experience.

I wasn't excited about reading thirty-three years of life in a small mid-western town (1930 pop. 1,013) where the activities of daily life were described without analysis or opinion. There was very little drama. Pete and his three siblings grew up in the shadow of our grandparents, even sharing a driveway between their respective homes. We never lived in Wayland but considered it our homestead, the childhood home of our father, our grandparents, aunts and uncle, cousins, and within a radius of 100 miles, relatives whose names we recognized and whose homes and farms we visited every year, but whose family connections we couldn't place with any accuracy.

Every summer we drove to Wayland for a two-week vacation. Though our father was an airline pilot, and we could have traveled to almost any *Trans World Airlines (TWA)* destination for little cost, our preference was to go to Wayland. We never flew. We always drove – two adults, five children, twenty baloney sandwiches, two roasted chickens, in a cooler, in a sedan. The drive from South Florida was 1,200 miles, driving straight through, never staying at a motel or eating at a restaurant. The return trip often included a cousin who would spend two weeks with us, and a bushel of blueberries or pecans purchased at a roadside stand along the way. There are no sure things in life, except the surety that our car would break down somewhere along the way. It was expected and never a surprise.

I promised Pete I would read the diaries and, within a week of our return to Colorado two boxes were delivered. The pressure was on. I put off the anticipated chore, arranging the journals in chronological order on the bookshelf and finally grabbing 1930. My first fears were realized: one mundane activity after another. What housework was done, what meals consisted of, who was visited and who came to visit, what church/civic events were attended, and where and when did people travel and how did they get there, what route did they take (detours were good for at least an hour's discussion upon arrival), and when did they return?

Something changed as the days, months, and years of the 1930s passed. I felt accomplishment as a journal was replaced and another was removed. I looked forward to discovering a family I was a part of but didn't really know. How many people get to see their parents while they were still in high school? My father was a high school junior in 1930, my uncle a graduating senior, and my aunt a freshman. It was fascinating to see how our elders evolved from adolescence to the people we knew in their familial roles. They almost looked like us. Each journal was filled with moments of anticipation and dread, interspersed with surprises, large and small, that kept the pages turning.

My grandmother said my father knew from age four he wanted to fly airplanes, declaring his desire one day while she was putting clothes on the line and pointing to a WWI vintage aircraft overhead. He was the youngest licensed pilot in the State of Michigan in the 1920s, hitchhiking twenty-five miles a day to Grand Rapids to take flying lessons and building hours, while still in high school. Starting with the 1930 beginning volume there is little mention about his passion, I am assuming because it was long past the point of novelty and a given that his love of flying was known throughout the community. It was who he was and who he would become. During one of our annual visits I walked "up town." I couldn't have been over the age of ten, when an elderly man approached, bent over, and stated: "You must be Max's boy." Both fearful and proud I nodded. "I knew him when he began. Tell him hello for me." He never told me his name.

Patterns and trends were not consciously referenced. Births, deaths, birthdays, weddings, funerals, and national and international events were valid only for the day they took place. Pearl Harbor, the fall of France, V-E and V-J days were accorded the same space as that day's church activities. The Great Depression was a fact of life embedded within almost every daily activity. Holidays were a one-day event. Thanksgiving and Christmas were rarely referenced prior to the day. Christmas seemed subdued in comparison to the current months of preparation and anticipation. Gift giving was modest. Linens and cookery dominated, with cash occasionally given to Grandma and Grandpa in surprisingly generous figures by appreciative family members.

The cumulative nature of happenings and references formed their own patterns. Our mother was befriended by Aunt Ruth and boarded with Grandma and Grandpa and was accepted into the family, but after a year the increased pairing of the once-separate activities of our eventual parents left little doubt a relationship was developing, with its culmination of a ring and a wedding two months later. Even though I knew better I began to wonder if they ever got married, but finally, with a few days to spare, the event was mentioned and took place. We were able to see how the family business evolved, the Reno Insurance Agency, that we took such great pride in visiting every year and seeing our name on the window.

We saw the steadiness of Grandpa Reno, rarely recognized or rewarded, the professional and civic growth of Uncle Phil who became mayor and president of the Michigan Municipal League, and had a street named in his honor, Reno Drive. For two weeks a year we were members of a prominent family, our annual visits always mentioned in the *Wayland Globe*.

Monday was washing and ironing day – all day. Every day was cleaning day. Chicken was what was for dinner, unless the fish were biting. The journals mentioned every outing and number and type of fish caught, not as a sport but as an economic and nutritional ledger. Doing nothing was a rare entry. Saturday and Sunday, for some reason, were always allotted the least amount of room on the page, with Sunday usually being the day of the week with more to observe and more to report: who attended church, who went to Sunday School, the quality of the sermon, the amount of the offering, and the multiple social events of the day that were church related. Church, social, and civic committees, societies, and clubs met throughout the week and were referenced throughout the thirty-three years of the journals. Offices were held and given up and held again.

Weather was a daily entry, especially in the winter when travel by automobile was a dangerous enterprise, based on the referenced accidents and fatalities. Unannounced visitations were a fact of life – desired, expected and reciprocated. They were not seen as intrusions and often resulted in additional meal guests. My father seemed to be the major culprit of the unexpected, arriving with a friend(s) in tow from Grand Rapids for food and shelter for a time to be determined. According to the entries, many of our father's friends became regulars at the house, to the point of stopping for a visit with father nowhere in sight.

Food and skills were bartered, and financial transactions, earned or spent, were recorded to the penny. The journals served as room and board ledgers ($3.00 per week in 1940). Listed were those who had paid their rent and who had not. It was surprising to see the number and frequency of people living in a house not designed for boarding but crucial to financial stability.

Although invaluable to my uncle and aunt as a babysitter for my four cousins, Grandma Reno never wrote the word "babysitting." The grandchildren were "visiting" or were "guests." When they were infants there seemed to be a direct correlation between their behavior and the length of their naps. They were sure to be described as "good" if they had taken a long nap.

For almost twenty years, going to the movies was a part of their week. Feature films changed two or three times a week and none seemed to have been missed. Grandma made it a point to list the title of the movie and a one- or two-word assessment: "cute," "I fell for it," "entertaining," and the kiss of death, "NG" (No Good). Two of the hundreds of films they viewed over the period from 1930 to the early 1950s gained her highest praise, earning two sentences of positive commentary: *Gone with the Wind* and *Mrs. Miniver*. The introduction of television in the early 1950s eliminated references to movies, with two or three exceptions when a biblical-themed film came to town.

Most impressive were the logistics of travel. Wayland was located between the cities of Grand Rapids (GR entry, 22 miles) and Kalamazoo (Kazoo entry, 30 miles). Everyone had to be somewhere, seemingly different, every day. Every day seemed to include a trip to GR or Kazoo, both planned and unplanned. Seven adults with two automobiles with separate destinations and different schedules. They managed to make it work, though there were unplanned overnight stays and taking advantage of anyone driving in their general direction.

The journals were a tease of mysteries, a jogger and corrector of memories, and a fount of the hard to imagine. That my father gave dance lessons is a picture impossible to conjure. We knew he was musical, made recordings with brothers who were professional entertainers, and was a disc jockey at a local radio station. It is something none of us had ever seen or imagined.

I called my sister to ask if she remembered our mother babysitting every evening after her fulltime job at the bank. A two-week visit by Grandma and Grandpa in 1959 had each day mentioning that after dinner Betty went to babysit. We finally decided our mother didn't want to admit we were in financial straits and had an evening job at Sears Town.

The more I considered the impact of the journals I was struck by the thematic connection to Thornton Wilder's 1938 Pulitzer Prize-winning play, *Our Town*, probably the most chosen selection for high school senior class plays across the country. I saw the role and manner of the omniscient stage manager in *Our Town* presenting the inhabitants and histories – past, present, and future, of a small New England town, and Grandma Reno's role as observer, editor, and recorder of our family history and the lives and culture of a small midwestern town, covering approximately the same time-period. What connects *Our Town* and the journals is their presentation of life as a linear progression of human events, behaviors, and experiences, as opposed to portrayals of meaningful singular events of popular novels and films. We are born and we die. We achieve and fail. We know joy and sadness. We often hear that historic merit stands on the shoulders of giants who came before. Our giants worked hard, overcame economic barriers, loved their families, looked after each other, and built and served their communities. We were expected to do the same.

The journals chronicled the evolution of my family that began with great social and economic promise, then a declining future due to the medical issues faced by our father. The love remained and our extended family was always there for support. My father and I were never able to resolve our adolescent-fueled differences before he died in 1962. I looked forward to seeing him after my overseas military service, realizing he was more than a father. He had a life before and beyond us, which the journals brought to life.

These observations now become the property of family members who would like to provide additions and corrections, and personal insights. The journals forced me to reassess what I had taken for granted. I had to start over, blessing those who silently wove the fabric of our collective lives. I fell in love with the family I thought I knew. I regret and ask forgiveness for all that was taken for granted, questions never asked, lives never explored, respect and compassion never given, and not acknowledging the sacrifices made for all who followed. Their impact is magnified by the fact that as we learned and were surprised, hovering over every entry was the fact we knew how it was going to end.

Humbly Submitted by Eric Reno
Son of Max and Betty
Brother of Alan, Judy, Tim, and Scott
Grandson of May and L.P.
Nephew of Uncle Phil and Aunt Fran, and Aunt Ruth
Cousin of Marcia, Pete/Lee, Denny, and Debbie

3. FAMILY: Phase I

Given the seismic changes of the last seventy-five years, I marvel at the domestic stability reflected within our families. As of January 2022, our marriages have lasted:

1. Brother Alan and Fran – 57 years
2. Eric and Patricia – 53 years
3. Sister Judy and Stu – 56 years
4. Brother Tim (deceased 2020) and Arlene – 43 years
5. Brother Scott and Kim – 49 years.

The duration of marriages is due to faith, commitment, understanding, respect, continued love, and forgiveness. We are in Kansas, Colorado, Florida, Michigan, and California. We have a biennial reunion over the 4th of July weekend. We have disagreements over politics and faith but have learned this is allowed, but gaining in intensity. We have gone beyond our love for each other. We genuinely like and seek out each other's company when possible. We glory in accomplishments and successes and feel the pain of disappointments and tragedies. We hope we have modeled for our children the family, civic, and religious values our ancestors modeled for us.

But we are a tale of two families. The three oldest siblings lived the early history, the pride, the economic and social advancement, the optimism. We saw the prime of our glamorous father, the warmth and immediacy of our wonderful mother. We knew we would get a new automobile every year and were surrounded by a stable environment, with a bright and predictable future. The three oldest children got the opportunity to express their musical talents, an excellent indicator of upward mobility. My older brother got piano lessons, discontinued after a year but resumed sixty years later. I was awarded an accordion, but could not manage the two-handed dexterity required. My sister took dance, but ceased after a few years. My two youngest brothers never got a chance. Their lack of interest and our social/economic decline precluded any more musical beginnings.

In our house we knew three dates: our birth dates, Christmas, and December 17 1903, when the Wright brothers undertook the first manned flight at Kitty Hawk, NC. As with most children, our fathers were our heroes, but ours was heroic beyond our household. Max Eugene Reno (1913-1962) was a pioneering aviator when aviators were heroic by the very nature of their fledgling profession. As children we were the envy of friends and classmates. The highlight of every week was when we drove to the Kansas City Municipal Airport to pick up our father when he came in from a flight. We would go to the viewing area on the roof of the three-story terminal and watch for the arrival of the *Trans World Airline (TWA)* DC-3. Our mother knew we had to be there to watch the landing as Captain Max Reno taxied up to the terminal, turned the plane parallel to the entrance, shut down the engines, slid back the side cockpit window, and waved to his then-three children.

A few years ago I was getting a haircut and listening to the conversation of a customer and his stylist. He was obviously a regular and was bringing his life up to date since his last visit. He announced the birth of his first born, a son. The stylist asked the date of birth and was told, December 17th. I debated, but finally asked: "Do you know the significance of December 17th?" He did not, but after being told and provided with additional historical information, he said he couldn't wait to get home to tell his wife. My good deed for the day.

My father's life was one to be envied. He was living his passion and lifting his family up the socio-economic ladder. Pilots bid for their monthly flying schedule, based on their seniority. Dad had high seniority and our mother said he bid Albuquerque when he wanted a good steak, Washington, D.C. when he wanted seafood, and New York when he wanted music.

It never occurred to me that parents and children had peer relationships. We loved each other but had our own circle of friends. My father was my father. He was not athletic, by interest or activity. My passion was baseball, from age six until I graduated from college. I cannot remember him ever asking how I was doing or what I had accomplished. I celebrated my rare moments of glory by myself. I remember the one time he attended a game. It was during the summer league when I was seventeen and scheduled to pitch a crucial game. Going into the seventh inning of a very close contest, in front of one of the largest crowds of the season, I saw him leaving to go home. He had never been interested; it was nothing personal. I don't believe I had a discussion with him about anything of depth. We talked, but the relationship was of adult to child, father to son. I never sought his counsel nor was it offered.

This discussion does nothing to diminish the importance of our mother and her steady, positive, and loving influence on my development and the well-being of our family. But my future lay in the eventuality of becoming a man, a husband, a father, a professional of some kind, and a breadwinner. My relationship with my father was defined by love, pride and adoration, pity and distance, regret, remorse, and selfishness.

The dynamics of our family changed dramatically when I was nine. We were all in the house on a Sunday afternoon and heard horrific sounds coming from the living room. It was our father having a *grand mal* seizure, rolling on the floor, foaming at the mouth, everyone screaming in terror. Neighbors rushed in, someone put a pencil between his teeth and over his tongue, as we learned later so he could not swallow his tongue. When the ambulance arrived and the attendants were taking him out on a stretcher, none of us thought we would ever see our father again. He was just thirty-eight years of age. Our lives changed on that day as we experienced a loss that would ripple through our family for the rest of our lives.

He survived but was grounded, not sure he would ever be allowed to fly again. He was able to retain aviation employment by becoming the head of Link-related training, the machines that simulated the handling and maneuvering of commercial aircraft. A few years later, and for reasons never shared with any of us, he resigned from *TWA*, with the promise of an executive position with Embry-Riddle Aviation, requiring a move from the only home we knew, Overland Park, Kansas, to Miami, Florida. The future was portrayed as one of beaches, boats, and Biscayne Bay. We started a boat fund, which topped out at $36.00. We (dad, mom, children ages 14,12, 9, 4, and 1) packed up, headed the 2,000 miles south for Florida, and got a room at a dilapidated motel near Biscayne Bay that featured blistering heat, humidity levels approaching the numerical temperature, and armies of land crabs roaming the barren grounds. Dad reported for work and was informed the person who promised him the job had been fired, and the job offer with it.

We stayed in the motel for a few weeks as our parents searched for our future. They finally found a house in Ft. Lauderdale, thirty miles north of Miami, with what we assumed was financial assistance from grandparents. I started to become aware of the financial concerns we were facing. From an early age the assumption was that we would all go to college, even though no one in our family had ever been. It was an expectation built into becoming rising middle class. Every cash gift we got for Christmas and birthdays went into our college fund. I told my mother they could have mine. She gave me a hug and said: "We already have."

A new neighbor in our new neighborhood, in our new State, was opening a gas station and offered our father a job, which he took. Two days into the job my mother went to see him at work and found him cleaning toilets. She told the neighbor my father was quitting. She couldn't stand to see him cleaning toilets for anyone.

For over a year our sole income was from the two jobs held by our mother: Woolworths in the day and Sears at night. My father loved music and could play piano by ear. It was his only interest or skill beyond flying. That was his day for two years. Every few months we traveled to Miami to visit two old friends from the Michigan flight school days. They had become pilots for *Eastern Airlines* and were living well in Miami Shores. They let it be known to my brother and I that, of the student pilots, our father stood out. When it came time to look for jobs they were successful immediately, but our father was turned down because of his height. He was only five feet, six inches tall. There was an informal, or formal, requirement: pilots had to be taller. Fortunately, the requirement did not apply to *TWA*.

One section of the meticulous scrapbooks lovingly designed and kept by our mother contained the accounts of our father's only documented "near miss." On July 16, 1943, he took off from Kansas City Municipal and one engine of the twin-engine DC-3 "swallowed a valve." They had just reached "V1 Speed," the decision speed for a takeoff or an abort. If he cut the power he faced a concrete dike ahead, holding back the Missouri River.

Had he continued the flight there was a good chance he would have crashed into the river or warehouses on the other side, fronting downtown KC. He cut the power and turned the plane on the rain-soaked runway, crashing into the concrete dike, destroying the wheel assembly system. He was suspended pending an investigation. The FAA conducted the investigation and out of it came praise from those aboard and a commendation letter for Captain Reno. We also have a letter from his co-pilot that states: "I still want to thank you for leaving that ship on the ground that morning." I asked my brother if any passengers were injured. He said the only passengers were two Army officers deadheading to New York City. The DC-3 was filled with crates of top secret Norden bombsights.

Two years after our move to Florida my father took a physical and was cleared to fly again. He got a temporary job flying for the Brooklyn Dodgers for the summer, and then was hired as a co-pilot for *Midet Airlines* (later to merge with *Mackey Airlines*), which consisted of one WWII vintage DC-3 and three pilots. The itineraries were Miami, Ft. Lauderdale, West Palm Beach, and Grand Bahama. Although he was hired as a co-pilot, his breadth of aviation experience far exceeded that of his co-workers, but in the airline industry seniority with the company is what counted. The job was a savior for my father and our family.

He enjoyed a beer and had been a moderate drinker his adult life. According to fellow pilots, pioneer aviators had a reputation as hard drinkers who could hold their liquor. When they got together my older brother and I silently took it all in. They talked and laughed uproariously about old times; barnstorming at county fairs, with wives and girlfriends portraying "fearless women" that would embarrass locals to spend $5.00 for a fifteen-minute ride in the vintage aircraft; air traffic controllers; near misses; storms of the century too large to go over or around; and the rare instances of co-pilots changing professions after one of those encounters. The beer flowed and the stories got better. Had you been a non-aviator you probably would have vowed to start using the train.

After his seizures, a beer or two changed his behavior from the father we idolized to a person we feared might be seen by friends and neighbors. His physical movements were unsteady, his words slurred, his facial expressions ugly. He would spend the evening in the kitchen playing forlorn music, and around 9:00pm would stagger to bed. His physical responses far exceeded his minimal consumption of alcohol. We never found out what caused the reactions. His *TWA* flying career ended because of the build-up of scar tissue in the mastoid and inner ear due to flying in unpressurized conditions when he had a cold. We assumed they were all related.

For four years I was creative in ensuring none of my friends came to our house if there was a possibility my father had been drinking. There was no problem the days he had a flight. It was when he didn't fly that consumed my day, hoping and praying he had not had that first beer. That was all it took. He felt the guilt, and I did everything, without word or action, to let him know my life was being ruined by his thoughtless behavior. Four years was a long time to hide and be angry. I didn't handle it well.

Scott, my youngest sibling by eleven years, and I recently talked about periods of family life. Out of it came his admission that he knew little about our father's drinking and knew nothing about our silent four-year adversarial relationship. He was born at the beginning of our financial and social decline and was only nine when our father passed away. It was a mistake to assume we had a common family history.

I do not have clear memories of what he was like as a father when we were very young, but somebody must have told me stories, abated my fears, put me on his shoulders, hugged and held me, dried my tears, dressed my skinned knees, taught me how to ride a bike, made sure we got the same Christmas presents as our best friends. At age eight I was rushed to the Emergency Room on Christmas Eve, in the middle of a party at our house, and into an oxygen tent because I could not breathe. He was always there. We were never without.

I've retained a memory for seventy-five years, its significance objectively insignificant. One evening I woke up and walked into our kitchen which had a snack bar and three bar stools. I must have been preschool age because I can remember looking up to see my father and older brother sitting at the counter eating cheeseburgers. I asked if I could sit with them, but my father said it was late and that we would have cheeseburgers at another time, just the two of us. We never did. I've lived with regrets my whole life and imagined scenarios where I would apologize, not requiring anything from him. I finally gave up my fanciful hopes, deciding I would have settled for shared cheeseburgers. I am also plagued by a memory I am unable to resurrect: I have no memory of ever hugging my father as an adult. I desperately hope I have just forgotten.

For the last ten years of his life our father was not a well man. He was the least athletic man I have ever known. He smoked two packs a day from an early age. One day in August 1962 I returned to our barracks after work and was preparing to go to dinner, when a colleague, who had been serving as NCO of the Day, stuck his head into our room and said he needed to see me outside. He was also a legendary gambler who supplemented his pay by being good enough to have a side business of loaning dollars at the rate of "five for four" (four lent, with five to be paid back on payday). He told me my father had died of a heart attack. He also said I was booked on a transport to New Jersey the next morning and had to leave early to get to the neighboring base that had aircraft. He said that if I needed money to let him know and there would be no interest. The trip from England to Miami gave me the time for grief and regrets and the practical questions his death presented to our family.

The funeral service was conducted by someone we didn't know, with comments general enough to apply to anyone. Those were not the days when family and friends were part of the ceremony and could testify and share personal relationships and experiences.

Or maybe we were too innocent and ignorant to know we could play a role. He deserved better. The service and the burial should have taken place in Kansas City or Wayland, Michigan. Florida is where we lived, but Kansas and Michigan were where he deserved to be remembered.

I had never considered the pattern of our lives. Our professional lifelines headed in opposite directions – our hopes, dreams, and accomplishments intersecting at approximately the same age, one descending and one ascending. My father's love of flying that provided the challenges and accompanying opportunities was taken away in his early forties. His health was never going to improve. His professional life reverted to his status twenty-five years previous. He was never going to fulfill his dream of flying jet aircraft. He didn't make it to age fifty. My educational career didn't begin until my early thirties, with my permanent administrative path beginning in my forties, providing a challenging and rewarding life for the next thirty years.

Our mother was the glue and heart of our family. Betty Jane Reno (1917-2007) never voiced her displeasure at our adult behaviors, beyond a stern look that firmly established her opinion. We never wanted to disappoint her by word or deed. If we did, we were silently forgiven. We did not receive material bequests, but we experienced and observed a lifetime of principles of behavior and character. She was a child of the Great Depression, from an upper midwestern family of six whose existence included multiple moves between agricultural labor and small-town commerce that never lasted. Schools were usually five miles away and transportation was by foot, in shoes whose tread was cardboard inserts, each lasting no more than a week. She was a hard worker, physically attractive and internally beautiful. Whatever athleticism we inherited was from our mother. She was in the middle of our softball games, loved to bowl, and took to golf, always accompanied by sister Judy, and played into her mid-80s.

She was a fierce protector of her children. At age seven I was accused by a clerk at the local five and dime of shoplifting a small wooden airplane. I had purchased it at another store with my allowance and was too convulsed by tears to make my case, even with my nine-year-old brother as a witness. After my tearful telling she ceased her chores and drove us to the first store, and after confirming the events, marched us down to the second, collected the owner, identified the culprit, and left the store with a publicly acknowledged and innocent seven-year-old.

But when we were not in the right we paid for our behavior. When I was eight years old I saw the boy from two houses away in our front yard. He was two years younger, and for some reason he was always being picked on – through no fault of his own. He was facing the street, and I ran out the door and pushed him down. I turned to go into the house and saw my mother standing in the doorway. She demanded an explanation. I had none. She didn't have to tell me how wrong I had been. That is why it is still so vivid in my mind seventy years later. She ordered me to go to the boy's house and tell his parents what I had done, why I did it, and apologize to our young neighbor.

Our side of the family was without business experience or intelligence. If we had been we would have avoided a decision that would severely damage the social and economic fabric of our family. In 1951 our father read an article about a large Air Force base being constructed twenty-five miles away, near a small town in Missouri. He calculated that the influx of thousands of servicemen/women and civilian employees would overwhelm the resources of the nearest towns. To take advantage of this economic opportunity we became the proud owners of the *JET* theater, a small, dilapidated movie house seating no more than 150 patrons. It was the only movie theater in town.

They chose the worst time in the history of the film industry to invest in a movie theater. Televisions were showing up in people's homes and gluing them to their recliners. The days of seeing every movie that came to town were gone, never to return. If my parents had asked a few probing questions they would have learned that military bases had their own theaters and charged admission at half the price of a town theater. Our mother went from a stay-at-home mother of four, ages 3-12, to managing and working six nights a week and multiple days to secure and return cannisters of 35mm film to downtown Kansas City. The family financial resources were drained and the pattern of family life we had grown into was torn apart. Whatever life presented, our mother accepted as her responsibility to address, never to avoid. From that point on she would work fulltime into her seventies.

She also carried a secret burden none of us were aware of. During the few years my father could not fly he would have periodic *petit mal* seizures. They would usually last less than thirty seconds. Consciousness was not lost but physical control was. They were terrifying to observe. I saw one. We were driving home and stopped at a light. I was in the front seat and told Dad the light had turned green. I looked over and he was staring straight ahead, not responding. My mother was in the backseat and said: "He will be OK in a few seconds." Cars honked and went around. After what seemed hours he put the car in gear, and we drove on. Years later, after his death and my return from England, my mother and I were talking about events I had missed while I was gone. I asked how long the *petite mal* seizures had lasted. In a quiet voice she said: "They never went away. I prayed every morning when he went out on a flight that nothing would happen. I told myself he was too professional to let a seizure take over. I also knew he had to fly." We never spoke of it again.

* * *

I was the second of five children: two boys, a girl, followed by two more boys. My older brother, Alan, followed in the footsteps of our father, and by age sixteen had saved enough money to buy a 1941 J-3 Piper Cub for $900. Dad was his instructor and by the time he graduated from high school he was flying an AT-6 (WWII single-engine fighter trainer) around Florida and the Bahamas to take aerial photos. The J-3 had a very limited dashboard. During an early sightseeing flight with my brother I asked how we knew when we were out of fuel? He yelled over the engine: "See that wire in front of the windshield? A cork is attached to the bottom. When the wire disappears, we are out of fuel." That was his after-school job. I decided that my job bagging groceries, though less romantic, included fewer risks.

After becoming a pilot for *TWA*, getting married, and having eight children, Alan bought half interest in a *Stearma*n bi-plane and chose aerobatics as a pastime. I wondered why he wanted to experience the thrill of near-death, and I held firm against the experience – not even a "snap roll," the straight and level flight with a corkscrew twist. Over the years I have impressed pilots I've met by knowing the technique of a *Lomcovak*, an aerobatic maneuver where a plane flies straight up and free-falls and tumbles from the point of power loss. They marvel at my courage. I let them know I never went past the role of observer.

I envied his passion and commitment, and the security of knowing what he wanted to do with the rest of his life. I also took pride in his accomplishments and bragged about him to schoolmates. We were two years apart, so we fought, got along, and fought again. But we were brothers. It wasn't until we became friends after high school that I had a family member in the stands when I was pitching. I was asked to be the best man at his wedding.

Our sister was everything you would want in a sister, a daughter, a wife, a mother, and a grandmother. She has had a long career as a "Mrs. Chips" at a private K-12 school, supporting the generations of leadership, doing what needs to be done, and greeting and ensuring that incoming students are welcomed and in the right place, many of whom were sons and daughters of previous generations of students.

She grew up between two older and two younger brothers. The brothers take credit for how she turned out. She was our mother's companion and best friend. Brother-in-law, Stu, was a scratch golfer, and it wasn't long until she went from golf widow to competing for Club Champion. Each of us, except Tim, took up the game at decade intervals. We never considered the game as children. Golf was a game for rich folks. We are now attempting to make up for the quarter centuries we did not play. Judy is still the best, and we try to keep up with her but are never successful, no matter how much we practice. Our annual golf outings, including the Will Reno Memorial, are events that mark the calendar the moment they are known. They are a joyful priority.

Brother Tim was our north woods representative. He served his country for six years in the Air Force as a B-52 Crew Chief and spent the remainder of his life loving to hunt and fish, and, along with Arlene, raising a wonderful family. He was quiet and thoughtful, and the furthest away. Though in regular communication, we did not get to see each other as often as we should have. When we did it was like we lived next door. He was a child magnet storyteller and the world's foremost authority on the *Three Stooges.* He left us too soon. He was the only smoker of the five siblings. I was best man at his wedding.

Baby brother Scott, the youngest member of the family, is a person of varied interests and skills. He is an accomplished surfer and the best natural athlete in the family. He is an entrepreneur, beginning by bluffing his way onto a construction site at age eighteen and soon becoming a foreman – void of any previous experience, and a young man who rose from driving his first nail to building one of the most respected construction companies in the Bay Area of California. His reputation includes not just the quality of his company's work, but also the personal and professional culture that permeates how and what they do.

4. ENDURING and ESCAPING ADOLESCENCE

A universal rite. How we survive is unique to our circumstances and character.

"Adolescence" is a term used to define our most awkward physical, social, and psychological stages of life, something to be endured, leading to adulthood and moments of maturity. It is not a condition defined by age. I was overwhelmed by raging hormones, and betwixt the forces of innocence and ignorance. As an adolescent I was vaguely and hopefully aware the best part of life was yet to come.

I wanted to be a man of the world: respected by the good, feared by the bad, and loved by the beautiful. I never took solace from contemporary icons of adolescent angst. The leads in *Catcher in the Rye* and *Rebel Without a Cause* caved too soon and were unconvincing victims of their creative middle-aged masters. I saw them as being too young for any lasting psychological and immaterial and lasting tragedy. Holden Caufield suffered but it was universal and temporary. I believed I was an adult-in-training and never expected to face the final judgement based on my callow youth. The interesting angst was yet to come, based on a life filled with adventure, risk, loss, tragedy, and moral dilemmas. Though seen in hindsight as a temporary phase, I've lived long enough to realize how much I underestimated the long-lasting, and unpredictable effects of my lost adolescence.

I wasn't a misguided youth. I was an unguided youth. I had an unremarkable childhood containing elements that steered my progress, punctuated by seemingly incidental moments that played a significant role in what we define as character. Even though I was an avid reader growing up, I focused mainly on the history and adventure from all centuries, requiring only an imagination, but never any analytical ability.

As I grew into adolescence I became an information sponge, absorbing current events and popular culture, never imagining this had anything to do with an education. I was subtly made aware of the world and its wonders by paying attention to the words and works of great minds and talents – the writers, artists, performers, musicians, and true statesmen and women who capture what is beyond our skills and imaginations, but not our hearts and souls. They explained what we didn't understand and presented what we didn't know existed. They were historic and current. My interest and exposure to the arts provided answers before I could formulate the questions. It was my responsibility to seek them out and pick their bones.

When I was a high school junior I read an article in *Esquire* magazine about Lawrence of Arabia, four years before he became an internationally known figure because of the film, the award-winning *Lawrence of Arabia*. His title conjured up romantic stories before I had read the first word. I might have been the only high school junior in the country in 1959 who owned T. E. Lawrence as a mentor of expectations.

Surviving adolescence in the 1950s was not a *Happy Days* script. Our 50th high school reunion was a last opportunity for many to see those who accompanied us through what we once thought were the most important years of our lives. Many attend reunions to reminisce and relive those years, but I attend not having much of any significance to relive. My interest has always been in people's stories: how did they turn out and how did the person they became compare to the person we perceived – by observation and interaction, reputation, or rumor?

Until age twelve I grew up in an environment void of the major social issues active in major parts of the country. Growing up in a small town in the center of the United States provided a geographic barrier against encroaching unpleasantries. Crime and violence existed in films and news reports, discrimination did not exist, possibly because there were no distinct groups to discriminate against. Doors were unlocked and friends and neighbors trusted. We had known our classmates since kindergarten and the unwritten rules of behavior and citizenship were understood and followed. I was admired and much sought after. I was a peer and class leader, held up as a model of social and academic behavior by teachers, among the first chosen for sports competitions, and co-captain of the Safety Patrol. No other belt and sash were consistently whiter, and no buckle shined brighter.

That comfort, security, and prestige disappeared when we moved to Fort Lauderdale, Florida, in 1954. The population increased 1000 per cent, the diversity multiplied, and the culture was foreign. I started junior high school two months late and was introduced to classmates during third period Geography. I stood outside of the classroom door for five minutes before knocking. I handed my registration paper to Mr. Ehrke, who looked and sounded like a former Marine, and who became a favorite teacher. He introduced me to a full class and seated me at a table in the front of the room next to his desk. He explained they were identifying countries by having the class shout out names when he pointed to the map. The class was quick to identify Canada and Mexico, the main countries of Europe, Japan, and China, and then he pointed to a large island off the east coast of Africa. I had joined in with the class right away and immediately shouted, "Madagascar." My solitary response started rumblings as to who said that, followed by whispers just loud enough to hear: "It was the new boy." Mr. Ehrke smiled and announced they were going to need to keep up with me. The bullseye was firmly attached. I completed my first day by informing the English teacher that her lesson on verbs was something I had already learned in Kansas. She indicated there might be a few I had missed.

As I became acquainted with the school and my classmates it seemed they were all from somewhere else, mostly the northeast: New York, New Jersey, and

Pennsylvania. They brought customs and attitudes far from those of Overland Park, Kansas. Swearing, using words that would have had me expelled from my previous school, was colorful and routine. Violence, in the form of after-school fights, was brutal and routine. Sexual rumors and realities were everyday occurrences. I had much to learn and understand. I was no longer in Kansas.

High school, and a sudden and new geographical and social environment, offered experiences I wasn't prepared for. When numbers turned to letters the six-year reign of the math king was overthrown. Everything was bigger and faster. Everyone seemed to have answers to the secrets of an adolescent existence. I was desperately seeking the questions. I was afraid, with no way to learn and no place to hide. My strategy was to become invisible in as many ways as possible. I dressed so as not be noticed. I didn't join and didn't contribute. I never initiated conversations and avoided any activity that could single me out. My strategy worked. I was never chosen nor recommended. I didn't have a significant relationship with a member of the opposite sex all through high school, and beyond.

But I did belong to an unofficial organization called the *Solid Blocks of Granite*, composed of second-year male Latin students so named by our exasperated teacher who would go down the row of desks attempting to get a knowledgeable response to her content questions. We were not disrespectful, just clueless. We began meeting the evening prior to every test and magically began to improve our grades, though we still had problems providing informed answers to oral questioning. We managed to survive our two-year sentence and continued to meet monthly for the remainder of high school. We rotated meeting locations, and I managed to avoid having meetings at my house, never knowing how my father would be feeling. We were a mix of types: mainstream college-bound, the confused, those hanging by a thread. We managed to stay in touch and over the years saw the *Blocks* become a college president, a noted environmentalist, a school superintendent, a college professor, and an international expert on Vietnamese currency.

5. BECOMING THE MAN

> "All the world's a stage and most of us are desperately unrehearsed." - Seán O'Casey

Following high school graduation I was so desperate for adventure that every weekend I would visit Port Everglades, which welcomed every flag of the world. I imagined the romance of visiting those siren-calling ports of call reflected in Joseph Conrad's stories and Bogart's films – all populated by memorable characters and exotic women in search of a strong and handsome protector.

On one of my Port Everglades visits I saw a Swedish freighter whose welcoming ramp tempted me to board. I asked a seaman where I might find the captain. I knocked on a glistening mahogany door and my preconception of what a Scandinavian Sea Captain should look like opened the door, inquired as to my business, and invited me into his immaculate and richly furnished cabin. He was tall, slim, with a neatly trimmed white beard, attired in white slacks and shoes, a blue blazer with brass buttons and gold braid. I told him I wanted to ship out to sea, and he asked about my vital statistics: age, skills, experience, and understanding of the life and expectations of a seaman. The last question revealed my naiveté and, in seeing his suppressed smile, my innocent ignorance. When I had finished he told me that I didn't want to ship out to sea, that I would be working with many of questionable character, and be disappointed by the less-than-exotic ports of call. He described the work as hard and boring. He told me to go home and seek adventure in a more constructive way. He escorted me to the door and wished me well.

My last idea for adventure was to fly to Brazil and follow the world hordes to the future capital of the country, to be called Brasilia. Brasilia was under construction in the heart of the Brazilian wilderness and people were flocking to get onto the ground floor of opportunities. This was more in line with the adventures of Conrad, though none seemed to have turned out well for most of his main characters. I stayed home.

My reality was less romantic: I had no money, was not considered to be college material, so I decided to try the world of adult work. My first job was with Florida Testing and Engineering. Contractors would bring cylinders and blocks of concrete to be tested for strength. My job was to put them under pressure until they shattered. I would record the level at which they exploded, then clean up the pieces. It didn't take long to figure this was not a long-range career opportunity.

My maturity and experience lagged my age, but in September of 1960 the acceleration began. Finally, and in desperation, I went to the Air Force recruiting office to complete the enlistment process I had begun earlier in the summer. When I graduated from high school the smart kids went to college. By not going to college I felt less than. Each year I spent in the military would mean I was that far behind those I envied. It never occurred to me the Air Force would provide guided maturity, academic achievement beyond any college classroom, self-confidence, pride, discipline, diversity, international exposure, civic awareness, and life-long friendships. It took a few years to realize my math and mind were faulty. What I gained was not a bad return on my four-year military investment. A minor consideration: I had gained a hernia from my concrete efforts and hoped Uncle Sam would pay for me to go under the knife, making me normal again.

All Air Force recruits were tested in four categories using a 100-point scale for each. The results would give an idea as to which technical school a recruit would attend after basic training. My scores were as follows:

MECHANICAL (15)
ELECTRICAL (55)
ADMINISTRATIVE (90)
GENERAL (95)

My Mechanical score guaranteed I couldn't be trusted within a mile of any aircraft, and my Electrical score showed I knew that light came from a switch. My score in Administrative conjured up visions of pencils and typewriters. But the General category was mysterious enough to activate my fertile imagination. It was the catch-all for general intelligence, revealing no apparent or specific skills. My score was good enough to have me tested for the aviation Navigator school. To my amazement I qualified – my first academic success in a long time. There was a catch: there were no vacancies in the program for a year, but if I enlisted would be contacted when a vacancy opened.

My re-education and social awareness began on Wednesday, November 9, 1960, the day after John Fitzgerald Kennedy was elected President of the United States. At the Miami Recruiting Office we were able to ask any questions that came to mind. Following lunch we raised our hands in allegiance. From that point on we weren't asked. We were told. I signed on the dotted line and began the four most developmentally important years of my life. I had a very recent four-year period of my life to backfill. I couldn't wait.

I had never interacted socially with a negro (terminology of the day) until I was seated next to a fellow recruit on a bus taking us to the Miami airport for our flight to San Antonio. He had graduated from Dillard High School, the "colored" high school in Fort Lauderdale and had never been on an airplane. Though we were from the same town there was no reason or opportunity for us to have ever met or conversed. It wasn't long until common futures gave us something to talk about during our three-hour flight. We also found a personal connection: he was Eugene, which is my and my father's middle name. Eugene was hoping to get into aviation maintenance; I shared that I didn't know what I wanted or was capable of achieving. We swapped rumors concerning what activities the next day held. None of our discussions reflected the societal and racial distinctions we had just left. We were two young, excited and frightened young men starting an adventure, ignorant of its challenges and our ability to survive them. By the time we landed in San Antonio I had my first post-high school friend.

We became members of a company, separated into four squads, each occupying a side of the two-story barracks. The four Squad Leaders were appointed on the second day. Ours came from central casting: handsome, athletic, college ROTC (Reserve Officer's Training Corps), with a commanding presence. A few days later he was gone. Four days later our Drill Instructors (DI) told us to form up and march back and forth until ordered to stop. I loved to march: straight and true, with my thumb and fingers aligned with the rhythm of my fatigue seams, able to anticipate all commands. We marched for half an hour and were ordered to halt and face the assembled DIs. A name was called. The new Squad Leader was introduced.

The recruits were the America I had seen on the big and small screens and described in print, representing a range of geographic, socio-economic, racial, ethnic, cultural, and religious backgrounds. Recruits were from the barrio, Hell's Kitchen, segregated communities, farms and factories, the coasts and heartland, with lives and experiences far beyond my delayed and sheltered adolescence. Most were older. I was an eighteen-year-old who could march. I was the new Squad Leader.

I was certain I was the least experienced in leadership, the least commanding, and the most terrified member of the squad. We never found out what happened to our previous leader. There were consequences of being the worst squad in terms of military protocols, assignments, and collective cohesion. I grew into my responsibilities and performed acceptably when the Drill Instructors were present. It was after lights out that I was tested. Friendships were formed and enemies made. Issues surfaced in the dark. One evening a simmering grudge threatened to turn into violence.

I threatened harsh punishments, unheeded, and knew if I didn't calm the situation someone was going to get seriously hurt and any question of my leadership ability would evaporate. I approached the would-be combatants to get between them and again threatened harsh punishment, silently shaking and terrified of the impending violence. Then a voice said: "You heard what the man said. Go back to bed. We need our rest." Eugene stepped forward and had the physical presence to disperse the squad to their bunks. It never happened again. Eugene was still there. I never thanked him.

The Air Force was everything I had hoped for, and much I had never considered. I didn't have to worry about being clothed, fed, having a roof over my head, or where my next paycheck was coming from. I distinctly remember a cold and rainy day in Basic Training in November, lying in a puddle of ice-cold water at the rifle range, attempting to qualify for a marksmanship ribbon, and thinking: "It doesn't get any better than this."

The sixth week of basic training was when we learned the future of our enlistment: where we were going and what we would be doing. Many in our company with good General scores were to become medics. That possibility did not excite me. I finally received my assignment: twenty-five weeks at Goodfellow Air Force Base in San Angelo, Texas, to become a Radio Intercept Analyst. I didn't know where that was or what that was, nor could the Drill Instructors provide meaningful details.

After three weeks at home, impressing my family with my new-found maturity, I boarded a flight to Dallas. I missed the last connecting flight of the day to San Angelo and took a local bus to the Grey Hound terminal and boarded my first commercial bus, an overnighter to San Angelo. My life of adult adventures was about to begin. Just before the door closed a young woman got on and hurried to the most remote seating available. An hour later I felt someone occupy the seat next to me. It was the young woman who asked if I minded her sitting next to me. She said her boyfriend had threatened to kill her and was afraid he might try at one of the frequent stops between Dallas and San Angelo. She fell asleep on my shoulder and slept well. I did not.

When I arrived in San Angelo the Sunday morning before the Monday report day I was expecting to be met by someone and delivered to the base. I waited for six hours and decided maybe they didn't meet every recruit, so I took my first taxi ride one mile to the base. I reported and was taken to my new home, a WWII-era barracks filled with students who were at all points of the twenty-five-week program. They were from everywhere and most were older and better educated, with at least two years of college. I tried to follow discussions but soon found out that in dealing with classified information, you learned how to talk without saying anything revealing, but confident your fellow students would know exactly to what you were referring.

No course materials could leave the classroom due to their confidential nature. We were tested every Friday. If a student failed any two weeks, he (I never saw a female analyst the whole four years of my enlistment) was reassigned and gone within a few days to other responsibilities at another location. If we made it through week number twelve we were marched to the secured compound to transition from *Confidential* to *Top Secret* materials. We stood at attention and waited for our names to be called. If called, we were allowed to enter the secured compound because we had passed an extensive FBI background check that had taken place during the previous twelve weeks. Those whose names were not called had failed the investigation for reasons only the FBI would ever know. They also would be gone within a week. At the completion of the twenty-five weeks the instructors brought a list of assignments into the classroom.

We knew that most would be international and knew previous classes had choices that included tours in northern Japan (southern Siberia), Turkey, Pakistan. Formosa, the Aleutian Islands, and San Antonio, but the assignments varied week to week. The three-year plum assignments – Germany, England, Scotland,

Italy, and southern Japan were usually reserved for those who had finished their initial one or two-year assignments elsewhere. Assignments were based on academic class rank. Of our class of fifteen I was ranked fourth. My two best friends, Hank Harrell and Bill Wooton, competed for first and second. Bill had a year of college at UCLA and Hank from a college in North Carolina. I envied and admired their experience, intelligence, and maturity, which they modeled and shared with me. I was honored to be their friend. I was beginning, starting with Eugene, a long history of choosing outstanding friends and mentors who guided my emerging character and allowed my occasional sophomoric behavior.

We had one day to make our selection. Our choices also included four slots in an advanced course lasting an additional fifteen weeks. The three of us decided to take a chance on the advanced training. At the end of the fifteen weeks I was still ranked fourth and Hank and Bill were still first and second. They brought in the assignments on the last day, and we could tell by the look on the faces of the instructors there was an issue. Could it be that bad? The Arctic Circle, Aleutian Islands, the Sahara Desert? One instructor said he had never seen such assignments for recent graduates in the two years he had been at the school. In addition to the usual suspects were four England assignments. Hank, Bill, and I had hit the geographic jackpot! I rushed to the payphone to call home to tell everyone I was going to England for the next three years. I knew my mother sensed my excitement, but I gave no thought to how she might feel about my being that far away for that long. She joined in my good fortune. For the next three years there would be no email, texting, cellphones, cheap transatlantic flights, only snail mail that would brighten the darkest day.

In February 1962, Hank, Bill, and I departed Maguire AFB, New Jersey, for England, with a stopover at the Azores for chipped beef on raisin toast and fuel, arriving in England at midnight. We were bused to our home base for the next three years, RAF Chicksands, and taken to a WWII-vintage Quonset Hut that had been used for storage the past five years. Cots and inches-thin mattresses were brought in. We were charged with cleaning the hut, setting up our bunks and making our beds, lighting the potbellied oil stoves, with the caution they had the habit of blowing up if the fuel lines weren't kept clear. Our priority was to get the stoves working no matter the danger. The glamour and excitement of my international experience had not yet kicked in.

We were to report for duty at 8:00am. The latrine and showers were two blocks down the road from our hut, and in the interest of time and efficiency everyone wore flip-flops and a raincoat coat over military-issued boxer shorts, no matter the weather, including blizzard conditions. Hank and Bill were assigned to different rotating flights within the 24/7 operation, and I was assigned to the Monday-through-Friday day shift because I wanted to play for the baseball team. Radio signals were weaker in the summertime, which would allow me to finish my smaller pile of intercepted traffic by lunchtime and play baseball in the afternoon. But the three of us remained friends for our three years in England and beyond.

RAF Chicksands had been a royal residence, a religious order (the Priory was established in 1152 and is said to contain the only remaining example of a Gilbertine cloister), a British military base, and a listening post during WWII where German radio traffic was intercepted and forwarded to the Bletchley Park codebreakers who successfully deciphered the German encryption machinery, labeled "Enigma." The base also had its own ghost. The story told was that in the 15th Century a pregnant nun was walled up in the priory. The offending monk lost his head. Sightings or hearings of Rosetta were scheduled for the third Wednesday of the month, usually reported by those who had closed the Airmen's Club, on nights that produced the famous English fog having two-foot visibility. The base had its own pond with swans and the reputation of being the most beautiful base in the Air Force.

Most of the base buildings and facilities were veterans of WWII. Quonset Huts were everywhere and used for every purpose. The vintage operations buildings housed the listening and administrative functions, and the antenna towers were original. Later that year modern dorms were built, the Ops functions moved to a large and modern building on the "Hill," and the multiple antenna towers were replaced by the latest in listening and direction-finding, an FLR-9 circular antenna that could contain four American football fields, and which provided a greater range of intercepts than their WWII predecessors. The antenna could be seen for miles and when asked by the locals as to its function, we replied that it was an "elephant cage."

My official job title was *Radio Intercept Analyst*, and sixty years later I am still reminded of the need to keep detailed responsibilities confidential. I was told by a former colleague that our mission was declassified in the early 1990s, but I have no official documentation. I would be communicating regularly with the National Security Agency (NSA), ensuring they had the most current information available and were alerted to any significant issues that might be reflected in the intercepted traffic. The analyst I was replacing had two days of duty remaining before he rotated back to the States after his three-year assignment. When I arrived for further orientation I was told my guide had gotten an earlier flight to the States and had departed with his three years of experience, leaving me with the stack of the previous night's intercepts. I became the resident expert before analyzing my first sheet of traffic. During the discharge process three years later I signed a pledge to not reveal the details of my work, nor travel to countries behind the Iron Curtain, and was made aware that violations were subject to incarceration at the federal prison at Leavenworth, Kansas.

The Cold War and threat of nuclear annihilation hung over our existence with the beginning of the Korean War. On October 22, 1962, we were instructed to listen to a special broadcast from President Kennedy. It would come on in our Quonset Hut at 2:00am GMT, October 23rd. We were told of Russian missiles in Cuba and the potential for nuclear war. We realized leaves would be canceled and our job as analysts was to detect signs of Russian activity on the island. I was under the added stress of being from south Florida. If war were to break out, my home and my family might be the first targets.

I usually gloss over my road taken after high school but now view my four years of military service in awe of what I took for granted. I faced unbending expectations of behavior and performance. I showed myself to be academically proficient in analytics and performed in the international arena at the height of the Cold War with independence and competence. I was nineteen years of age. Not bad for a former concrete smasher.

I loved my job, learned my responsibilities, and earned the respect of my colleagues, some of whom were twice my age. Many were career military and had been posted all over the world. Many had families and others were on their way. I was told that three-quarters of the airmen who arrived single left married by the end of their three-year tour. That ratio seemed about right: most first termers were young, spoke the same language as their delightfully attractive hosts, and were rich by European standards. I was also tempted, but my beautiful best friend and I were too young, unformed, and I was desperately in search of my dream with no substance.

Not long after I arrived I was invited to go with a group taking Joe to London. He was scheduled to rotate home after his three years and had never been to London, forty miles to the south. I wish I could say this was an isolated event, but it was common to find international exposure for many was limited to surrounding communities, and the on-base Airmen's Club. Every Monday morning I would be asked where I had gone and what shows I had seen and where else I had been. Though asked with good humor, the envy and curiosity of many were sadly obvious.

The following 2017 letter is a reminiscence that attempts to capture the significance of the events of my military time, and its profound and extended influence over my life.

May 17, 2017

Hello Pete and Gina: (Pete/Lee Reno, 1st cousin, and Gina were early Peace Corps volunteers in Liberia. That, and their accomplishments since have made them role models for a long time.)

Have been meaning to write since Pat and I watched the movie *Jackie* the other evening. The tremendous heights of optimism and depths of tragedy of those four years rose to the surface. I remembered the feeling of universal optimism and the role we wanted to play in achieving social change. One instant on one day revealed a sobering truth: there were forces capable of manipulating the world – far beyond our ability to comprehend or control. Little did we know this would be revealed, in the extreme, fifty-three years later. Though much good was accomplished we may not have understood the rate and progression of social and political change. I think we believed change would be evolutionary, with future generations embracing and refining the positive dynamics of previous generations. What we didn't comprehend was each generation's need to make its own mark, and the collective amnesia that seems to set in down the evolutionary road – not knowing, understanding, or caring what has brought us to this point. A few years ago a colleague asked when I knew it was time to retire. When the latest brilliant educational movement/innovation comes around for the third time, it's time to retire.

Enough philosophy. On to nostalgia. We were so blessed to have been our ages at that time. I learned more about my country by being absent than I would have by being there. We were envied by all, the world's greatest nation, led by a rock star and his beautiful and cultured wife. We could do no wrong. The events we saw and experienced! When asked, I tell folks I was in the military when the Berlin Wall went up, the Cuban missile crisis, the MLK-led March on Washington, the Kennedy assassination, and the Beatles. The last fact impresses them most. More poignantly, where we all were when we heard about the President. My two roommates were in Paris and, speaking no French, saw a passenger on the Metro reading a newspaper with a picture of LBJ with a raised right hand and Jackie standing nearby in a stained suit. They rushed to find the nearest *International Herald Tribune.* I was listening to the radio, attempting to refine my beginning German language skills and heard the words "Kennedy" and "*tod*" (dead) together, followed by the masculine hysteria of old boys and new men throughout our dorm.

I had tickets to see *Hamlet* at the National Theater on November 23rd, the night after the assassination, and was debating whether I should go. I got on the train and went, feeling as alone as I have ever felt, wondering why I had not stayed with grieving colleagues. The audience was truly subdued, all were affected no matter their country of origin. At the end of the performance the cast came out (including Peter O'Toole as Hamlet), and we prepared to stand for the traditional playing of "God Save the Queen." One of the cast members held up his hands to get the audience's attention and said: "Please stand and join us in paying tribute to the President." What followed was the playing of the "Star Spangled Banner." I did not hear one word as the audience emptied into the street, only sniffles and sobs.

I miss our annual trip to Washington and seeing the both of you. I always looked forward to our conversations – fueled by wonderful food and drink and your welcoming hospitality. I've admired your lives for more than fifty years and always consider how emblematic you both are of that brief, life-defining flash of time. If you have not yet, watch *Jackie*. Let me know what you think.

Rick (family nickname)

What a surprise when America was invaded by the British. When we arrived in England in 1962 it seemed as though seven of the top ten popular songs were by American artists, according to *Radio Luxembourg*. There were great English performers, many given titles such as the "English Elvis." We assumed that was the way of the world. We did not accept English fashions; we were Americans. Their hair was longer, their clothes fit tighter, their shoes more pointed. We had more money and the most charming world leader and the most beautiful First Lady.

In 1962 we started hearing about a musical group called the *Beatles*, and fell in love with their music. We could not wait for their next song and were never disappointed. They were different, they were special. When we heard they were going to America we were concerned they would be laughed off the stage because of their long hair and funny clothes. We were off in our prediction. In July 1964, when I was processing my discharge at McGuire Air Force Base (New Jersey), the only music I heard was the Beatles. American hair had gotten longer. The British Invasion was underway. I became a minor celebrity for having been there.

I was scheduled to get out of the service in November 1964 and begin college in January. In May I sent my weekly report to the National Security Agency (NSA), summarizing issues of interest and updates, including the description of a complex issue I had resolved. A few weeks later I received a letter of commendation citing the quality of my analysis and an offer of civilian employment at NSA's headquarters at Ft. Meade, Maryland. The offer included doing challenging work I understood and was good at and living close to our nation's Capital. I turned down the offer. I was still committed to becoming our family's first college graduate, and having the "collegiate experience." My decision to turn down NSA's offer is still puzzling to me. I chalk it up to a form of homesickness and an ignorant understanding of what constituted the "collegiate experience." I could have worked at NSA and gone to school – something that never crossed my mind. This would not be the last of my less-than-considered life decisions.

My decision to turn down the offer from NSA was also influenced by the death of my father while I was away. I would become "the man of the family," supportive of my mother and a father figure to my younger brothers. Tim (15) and Scott (11) would benefit from my experience and maturity. I would be someone to look to for guidance. I would ensure they avoided my missteps: the decision-making, idleness, lack of academic focus, choice of friends, missed opportunities. My intentions were noble, but implementation proved I was not ready for enlightened parenthood. If they had thought of it, I believe they would have mowed every lawn in the county so they could have purchased a one-way ticket back to England for me.

I underestimated the ease with which I would be able to transition to civilian life where I faced an uncertain future that included no financial resources. There was no G.I. Bill at this time that had provided higher education benefits for veterans of WWII and the Korean War. That wouldn't be available for another two years. I wasn't entirely sure as to whether I was truly college material, and no understanding as to career or professional interests. In a matter of days I went from using my *Top Secret Codeword* clearance to monitor and analyze intercepted communications, to living at home and stocking shelves at the local A & P grocery store.

My questionable judgement began on my second day home. The UK was a great place for auto enthusiasts, discovering automobiles they had only read about or seen in movies, newsreels, and magazines. They were abundant and reasonable. In my three years in the UK I was in an automobile three times, for short distances. I wanted what I had never experienced: buses, trains, and the London Tube. That's where places were discovered, strangers were met, history came alive, and adventures began.

Reality hit when I returned to Florida. I was carless. On my first civilian day I visited a car lot and returned with my first car in four years. The next morning I looked out to our driveway and saw the ugliest automobile ever designed – a 1958 brown sedan, manufacturer easily forgotten. That day I returned the metallic lump to the lot and traded it in for a 1960 white MGA convertible, my mechanical partner through college and my expensive tie to the country I loved and desperately missed.

6. The BEAUTY of the SEXES

Attractiveness is given. Beauty is earned.

In the mid-1990s my wife, Pat, handed me a paper announcing Chanel was bringing out a new fragrance called *Allure,* and there was a contest requiring applicants to describe what makes a woman alluring, in twenty-five words of less. She encouraged me to enter. I submitted the following:

> Her whole being says,
> "I am confident in who I am,
> And wouldn't you be fortunate
> To be a part of my life."

To everyone's amazement I came in second, statewide. We received two front-row tickets to the show, *Sunset Boulevard,* opening in Denver.

* * *

Detours to ignorance and stupidity abound as we traverse the pathway from innocence to maturity, praying they do not prove to be fatal. I survived, but the journey was littered with false starts, interesting stops, and final good fortune. My solitary good friend during our senior year of high school, Tom Kerr, had a car and every Friday night we would cruise the hot spots hoping against all previous success to find girls who might be interested in us. One Friday it happened: two attractive young ladies from a rival high school accepted our invitation. I wasn't sure what to do or say, and one girl indicated we weren't what they were hoping to find. As they got out of the car one of the girls nodded in my direction and asked: "Does he talk?"

The advantage of seeing the opposite sex as a great mystery made the discovery of differences even more exciting. Growing up in Overland Park, Kansas in the mid-1950s was a perfect time and place to show how sheltered and ignorant many of us had been, deprived as we were of current television that exposes all ages to the secrets of the sexes. "Darn" was about as rough as it got. Most of us had grown up together, attending the same schools and experiencing the same social environment. That is why the 6th Grade boys wondered why the 6th Grade girls were scheduled for special monthly afternoon meetings during the Spring term – no boys allowed. We talked it over and came up with our own theories, ranging from what girls need to know about junior high school, to what every girl needs to know about baby-sitting. A classmate who had an older sister who had attended the meetings the previous year volunteered to educate us after school, off school property, if we swore never to reveal our source. We thought the school day would never end, and when we did rendezvous had 100% attendance. The mystery was about to be revealed.

According to our expert, at this stage of our lives certain physical changes were taking place. We grimaced and indicated we were not idiots. He looked at us and said: "But do you know what happens to girls?" No one wanted to take the chance of being wrong in front of peers. "Well, here is what happens. Girls start growing breasts and the growth makes them bleed." Finally, things started to make sense. You could understand how the force of that growth against their chests would affect the flexibility of the skin. Confident we were now part of an elite group with privileged information, we spent the remainder of the 6th Grade looking for telltale signs of blood on blouses. No one ever admitted to never seeing anything.

My four-year high school monkish adolescence was defined by my fear of being found out. Getting close to people meant visiting other homes and families, while my home was off limits, never knowing my father's condition. I would occasionally develop an in-class relationship with a member of the opposite sex that would end when class was dismissed. For four years I observed and envied the romantic relationships of classmates, wondering when I would be a participant. The closest I came was the end of senior year and the approach of the Senior Prom. I had established a friendship with a young lady who seemed interested in me, and who I had heard was dateless for the Senior Prom. I had never asked anyone for a date. I agonized, but did nothing.

During the last week of high school a day was set aside to have Class Yearbooks signed. Many of us had been classmates for six years. I attended, asked for signatures, and contributed baseless tributes to those who asked. When I got home I read other people's versions of my comments and was anxious to find any of significance. I finally found a note from my in-class friend and potential Prom partner: "To Eric Reno, the nicest boy I've met at Stranahan High School." It kept me warm for weeks but wasn't much to show for four years of social solitude.

Although high school offered no relief from my monastic life, the military offered possibilities I had never imagined. I had four years of solitude and masculine development to make up for. I was in a hurry. I was desperately hoping my new international environment would reward me with romantic opportunities all those around me seemed to be enjoying. I didn't have to wait long. We landed in England on a Friday in February 1962, and learned we had the weekend to ourselves. With London forty miles away, Hank and I decided to see one of the great cities of the world. We went to the bank to convert our accumulated pay into pounds sterling and got our first taste of a truly foreign world. A *pound sterling* was worth $2.80. The coinage required reinforced pockets and a new vocabulary: *Shilling, Half Crown, Sixpence, Florin, Ha'penny (half penny),* and *Guinea.* Pound notes were twice the size of dollar bills, and a penny seemed to be the size of a silver dollar.

We stuffed our pockets and dressed in a way that hopefully wouldn't give us away as being fresh off the boat. Having grown up in south Florida I was poorly equipped to look native. I hoped my first sartorial purchase after learning I was going to England would provide camouflage – my lined London Fog raincoat, the kind my cinematic hard-boiled heroes wore. Our cover was blown when we got on the bus to Bedford in search of the train station. We held up a line of passengers as we attempted to identify which coins made up the fare into town. Additionally, our short hair, white sox, and rounded-toe shoes were immediate giveaways as to nationality.

My pre-arrival perception of what I might expect on my first trip to London was that it should be gray, cold, and overcast, preferably with a thick fog. I was not disappointed. I had a lifetime of sunshine. Sunshine had no character, no mystery. I soon realized my lined raincoat may have made me look like a sixteen-year-old "hard-boiled" but offered very little warmth against an English February.

That evening I took my first train ride to anywhere, but the destination made it a multi-experiential event. Everything was an eye-opening first. Where to? Piccadilly Circus of course! We managed to navigate our first Tube ride from King's Cross to Piccadilly. We emerged from the station and were engulfed by a mass of international bodies, looking and speaking outside of our combined forty years of life experience. But it was also familiar. We had seen this neon center many times in cinema, newsreels, novels, travelogues, and postcards. We were there but weren't sure what to do next. It was early evening and freezing. We remember being told that, despite being a major city of the world, London pretty much shut down at 10:00pm. We found a Lyons Corner House for food and decided to visit another oft-whispered area of the city, Soho, knowing the British Museum and the National Gallery were probably closed.

We found our way to Soho, another neon neighborhood with a consistent message: "If you have money, we have girls." Both sides of the street had "clubs," with a carnival barker inviting strollers to look at pictures of the beauties inside and encouraging us to come in because "the show was just about to begin." This was my first sample of the fleshpots of the world. The closest I had ever come was when two classmates and I were attempting to work up the courage to buy tickets to see Brigette Bardot in *And God Created Woman*, the first R-rated mainstream movie to play in Ft. Lauderdale. The film had all the elements we had only read about: it was French and starred an actress who had passed the sexual limits of Marilyn Monroe.

Up to that time of our lives the limit of consummated sexuality, as allowed by Hollywood censors, was a passionate kiss, followed by the smoking of cigarettes. We were sixteen and spent a half-hour walking up and down the sidewalk, making sure no neighbors were in the area who would report us to our parents and the police. We had been told by a classmate to watch for the shower scene when Bardot stepped out of the shower and dropped her towel. With great courage we purchased tickets and with great anticipation we saw the scene developing. At the "moment of the towel" there was a mechanical malfunction with the projector that blurred the epic scene. They were right. You would go blind!

We chose the Florida Club in Soho. The irony was not lost on me. The moment we entered the club we met and were escorted to a table by four attractive young ladies, with drinks appearing two at a time and pound notes disappearing at the same rate. We asked when the show was going to start – always soon. Hank finally saw we were being fleeced and made a move to see the manager. In a moment four very large men in shiny silk suits and slicked hair started for our table. One of the girls indicated she had things under control, and they retreated. She apologized and told us they were having a party at her place after the club closed and wanted us to come. She said to come back at 10:00pm when the club closed, wait across the street, and we would all walk to her flat.

We froze for the next two hours exploring a London we vowed to never return to without more preparation. At 9:30pm we positioned ourselves across from the club, shivering from anticipation and weather. I shifted from foot to foot, hoping to keep the blood flowing, and looking down an alley at a neon tower advertising a play titled, *Stop the World, I Want to Get Off.* After thirty minutes of repetitive flashing I vowed to see the play but never did. A blonde in her thirties appeared on the block and walked back and forth past us a few times. The third time she stopped, asked for a light, and asked why we were standing in the cold. Our story elicited a shake of her head and small smile and the comment, "They won't come out." We assured her they would. They had promised. She continued to the end of the block, and we could see her in conversation with a man who had just appeared. After a few minutes she came back and said that if the party didn't work out to give her a call and she would come back to pick us up. She gave us her phone number and said, "Give me at least an hour before calling."

At exactly 10:00pm a large black sedan pulled up in front of the club. The doors opened, the girls jumped in, speeding off into the freezing night. Hank and I looked at each other hoping we still had the phone number. We waited the hour and spent a half hour looking for a pay phone and learning how to use it. We had not asked her name but described who we were. We could hear a muzzled laugh. She said her name was Lilly, and she would pick us up in a taxi in fifteen minutes. True to her word Lilly arrived and we returned to her basement flat. She fixed tea and scrambled eggs and told us her story while we ate and defrosted. She didn't want us to get the idea she was a professional. She was a civil servant in the navy and needed money to help her mother. From our brief conversations across from the Florida Club she saw we were in trouble, easily reading our urban ignorance.

In the morning she made breakfast and took us on a brief tour of the historic London and delivered us to King's Cross railway station to make sure we wouldn't be AWOL on our third day in the UK. Hank went to get tickets, and I thanked Lilly for being so kind and generous. She said it had been a pleasure to meet us and that I should come back to London soon, by myself. I stammered a response, received a kiss on the cheek and a welcoming goodbye. I was not sure what to share and what to do with the invitation. As usual, I did nothing.

Once I started my new professional responsibilities I established a routine every morning prior to reporting for work, getting coffee at a refreshment stand before entering our secured facility. One of workers was a young and beautiful Jamaican girl who smiled and beguiled us with her island accent. She soon learned my order and my name, greeting me with both every morning. Our exchange of "good mornings" grew longer and more personal. Every day I looked forward to seeing her until she made it clear she was interested in more than counter chat. I panicked, being too recent from a segregated world. I started getting my coffee elsewhere and despised my cowardice.

In January 1963 my international manhood journey took me to Frankfurt. I was chosen to attend the University of Maryland's Heidelberg Campus for the first three months of 1963, to study German language and history, resulting in the awarding of fifteen college credits.

My introduction to my new home began on our first evening in Frankfurt. No one in our group had been in a non-English speaking country, so we sought out familiarity. A movie theater across from the *Hauptbahnhof* advertised a John Wayne movie. Our comfort level disappeared in John's first scene: he rode up to a gathering, jumped off his horse, raised his hand – and in a non-John Wayne voice shouted, *"Wie geht es ihnen?"* From that beginning I found myself enthralled a month later by watching *Madame Butterfly* at the Wiesbaden Opera House. I could not get enough of the new, different, and sophisticated.

We had language in the morning and history in the afternoon, after which we would take the train into Frankfurt to apply the language lesson while it was fresh in our minds. The lesson concerning the train station took us to the Frankfurt *Hauptbanhof*. We attempted to pass for natives and asked in our newest and best German, *"Wann ist der nachste Zug nach Wiesbaden gehen?"* The answer was usually immediate: "The next train to Wiesbaden is at two o'clock. *Nachste bitte.*"

The three months in Frankfurt was a submersion in recent history. The infants in WWII were the new generation of German youth – raised in a western, democratic environment. Fascism belonged to their parents. In the early 1960s Frankfurt was completing the reconstruction of the city, though the architectural dominance of the IG Farben industrial complex and its role in supporting the infrastructure of the Holocaust was known, but little understood. Faded uniforms, minus identification or decorations, could still be seen on the street. But youth prevailed, jazz clubs seemed to be everywhere, and the night life seemed more active than it had been in London.

Our history courses were more than interesting. They were taught by a German gentleman who fought on the Eastern Front in WWII. We never met anyone who fought on the Western Front. He was an excellent teacher and provided historic facts, insights, and opinions we had never heard of or considered. By the end of the course I was a champion against Germany's unfair treatment at the end of WWI.

Fellow students were from bases all over the European theater and included enlisted personnel, officers, and some dependents. I became friends with Jack, my age, level of sophistication and temperament, who was based in Turkey. In February he told me he was taking a long weekend to Paris to visit an expatriate aunt he had never met and who had been in Paris since 1940 and taught at the Paris Conservatory of Music. He asked if I wanted to go with him and got his answer from the immediate grin on my face. Life just kept getting better and exceeding my hoped-for adventures.

Our train was to leave Frankfurt at 2:00pm the next Friday and get us to Paris at 9:00am the next morning. It was the milk run. On our departure day we were dressed in our finest and put everything into one large suitcase and one overnight bag. We got to the station an hour before departure and saw a train on our track. It seemed quite full, so we decided to board while good seats were still available. We threw the full suitcase overhead, and Jack went to make sure the train was leaving on time. I heard a "chug" and felt a slight movement. Jack ran into our compartment, grabbed the overnight bag and yelled: "This isn't our train. This train is going to Wiesbaden. Let's get out of here!" I got up, wrestled with the large and heavy suitcase, and ran to the closest exit. The train was gaining speed and Jack was running alongside yelling: "Throw out the suitcase and jump!" I threw, jumped, and rolled fifteen feet, head over heels. Jack rushed to my side to see if I was OK. The blood had drained from his face, which made me wonder if the suitcase had been damaged. He helped me up, brushed me off, and pointed to the end of the platform six feet away that dropped four feet onto the rails. He then pointed to a steel pole in the other direction and said I had missed it by inches when I had jumped off the train. I still shudder knowing a life-threatening event was only inches away.

There was little sleep during the trip and its twenty stops. My exciting train exit left me feeling as though I had just crawled out of a dust bin, but the constant movement of languages and cultures on the slow-moving train was part of our education.

We arrived in Paris and found a hotel and were scheduled to meet Aunt Louise at her favorite restaurant that afternoon. The Eiffel Tower was closed due to rumored threats related to the recent Algerian War. We rushed to Notre Dame and the Louvre where the out-of-world realization hit me. When we walked into the Louvre the first work of art I saw was the Venus de Milo in the middle of the entrance aisle, the perfect introduction to Paris and a world miles away from every place I had ever been.

At 4:00pm we stood outside the entrance to French cuisine, attempting to make sense of a menu we couldn't read. There was a large outside dining area lining the main street – too cold for us to use but picturesque enough to mentally populate the tables with attractive and fashionably dressed Parisians. It was early enough that we essentially had the restaurant to ourselves. Aunt Louise was at her table and rose to welcome us, delivering continental kisses I wasn't sure how to return. Jack and Louise shared family stories, and I felt honored to have been included. We learned Louise had been in Paris since 1940, arriving before the occupation of France by the Nazis. That time has since become one of my favorite historical periods of study, and many years later realized the lost opportunity to discuss those years of her life.

Aunt Louise saw our struggle with the menu and offered translation services and recommendations. We both asked her to order for us, an offer she willingly accepted. I had my first glass of wine and fell in love with our first course, *escargot*, overcoming my initial hesitancy and convincing myself that French snails must be a different breed from those on American sidewalks. I never knew chicken could taste so good or that a meal could be such an elegant event. We finished with *petite fours* and an *aperitif*. If I had smoked I would have lit a cigar.

Louise said she would love to show us Paris nightlife but was giving that responsibility to her niece, from her husband's side of the family, who was to meet us at the restaurant. Within minutes the most beautiful woman either of us had ever seen entered the restaurant. Jack and I looked at each other, silently acknowledging this was the Paris we had hoped for, and hoping she was family. She walked past the rows of tables and didn't stop until she came to ours. We were introduced to Michelle.

I had seen a Michelle only in movies, in a full-length fur coat, perfectly made up, in a dress that enhanced every part of her, and a smile that indicated she was looking forward to the evening. The problem we faced was that Michelle spoke little English, and we spoke no French. Aunt Louise didn't think this would be a problem. She said that Michelle was a great communicator in any language. We agreed, not knowing why. We thanked Aunt Louise for a memorable evening, an unforgettable meal, and her informative and stimulating conversation.

When we reached the sidewalk Michelle put her arms through each of ours and began our evening, escorting us through Montmartre, the most Parisian of neighborhoods, where the artists were painting and selling, and the streets guided us through the picturesque elevations of the 18th *Arrondissement*. Our first stop was a club pulsating with music and young people with different languages, facial features, color, and fashions. We found a large table with three vacancies and ordered drinks. Directly across was a party of Asians, and we attempted to start a conversation. Jack said he had been stationed in Formosa for a year. Our table neighbors made it clear they were not from Formosa, but mainland China. I wasn't sure I should be talking to Communists, fearful my security clearance would be pulled if anyone found out with whom I had spent the evening. I could be reassigned to a location you couldn't find on the map. They looked normal, but

I wasn't sure what I expected Communist Chinese to look like.

Our next stop was a club where dancing accompanied the drinking. I attempted to explain that I could not dance. I had been labeled by those who had seen me try as being "beat deaf." But Michelle was most persuasive, and Jack and I fell into a pattern of alternating as her dance partner. I got more proficient with every glass of wine and fell more in love with every song. Late into our evening Michelle and I got a slow song. We had mastered communication without language, and she suggested we leave for the evening. I feebly protested that I could not leave my good friend by himself, with no explanation. She gave me a hug and we returned to our table. Jack's turn. I didn't see him until 10:00am the next morning. I forgave him. It was his trip, and I was his guest.

I must digress and explain a comment from a prominent baseball figure named Leo Durocher. He was a fiery character as a player and manager in the first half of the 20th Century and ended up in the Baseball Hall of Fame. You can find a list of his sayings such as: "I've never questioned an umpire's integrity. Only his eyesight." But the one he is most known for having supposedly said is: "Nice guys finish last." I've always associated that saying with how my Paris trip ended. I thought there might be a lesson somewhere in my chivalric decision.

Jack and I finished our Paris trip on a delightful note. We had an express back to Frankfurt and planned to use our time studying for our language test scheduled for the next day. We had proven we were not natural linguists and traded butchered words and phrases back and forth. We had a whole car to ourselves until the German border when we were joined by a small and elderly woman carrying a large mesh bag filled with food and clothes. She looked exhausted, and we would have to lower our voices.

A half hour later we could see she was awake and attempting to suppress a smile after each attempt to master our new language. Finally, she sat up and yelled, *"nein, nein,"* and began laughing at our every attempt. We joined in and exaggerated our ignorance, which brought tears to her eyes. She spoke no English but truly attempted to help us with our studies. Finally, we all gave up, got three glasses of wine from the dining car, and shared some of the wursts and cheeses she had in her bag. For not being able to converse effectively we all had a wonderful time. She got off at the next stop, thanked us (*dank*e) for the entertainment, and laughed her way off the train.

* * *

After my return from Frankfurt, my roommates, Frank Fitzpatrick, Rick Busch, and I rented a flat in Barons Court, one Tube stop west of Earl's Court on the Piccadilly Line. We worked different shifts so it was rare to be in London at the same time, but Rick's and my off days coincided, and we had tickets to see *My Fair Lady* at the Theatre Royal, Drury Lane, adjacent to Covent Garden, when that area would have been recognized by Eliza Doolittle as her place of work. Our bed-sitting room was on the first floor. Rick had met our neighbors across the hall, a nurse and a dancer, and informed me we had been invited to a party they were having that weekend and would need to bring our own refreshments. My first BYOB (Bring Your Own Bottle) event. Rick recommended getting Johnnie Walker Black Label Scotch at the Base Exchange, a choice he knew wouldn't be matched.

The party was well underway when we got back from the play. We carried our Johnnie Walkers across the hall and saw we were overdressed. We were the only suit coats, starched shirts, ties, and shined shoes in the room. We set our bottles among all the others, poured a drink, and began to mix. Rick slipped into conversations with ease, and I looked for a spot where I could stand without drawing attention but appear that I belonged. I walked into the kitchen where two women were engaged in a conversation made clear was for them only. One of the women was visually striking, full makeup, in a black dress and high heels, dressed for a more elegant party. I gulped my drink and went back to replenish it and saw the two Johnnie Walkers had passed away. The popular siblings had led frighteningly brief multicultural and distributive lives.

The attendees covered all areas of commerce, the arts, nationality, political persuasion (socialist, communist, anarchist), religious conviction or not. A boarder I had met briefly asked if I was enjoying myself. He said I might like to meet a countryman from Cleveland. I felt relieved to finally meet someone with a common background. I was introduced to a woman who did everything possible to hide the fact she was an American from Cleveland. She didn't look American, talk American, think American, or like Americans. Our whole brief discussion of "back home" took place as her head swiveled in search of an alternative to me. Within minutes she excused herself and found an alternative with an accent.

My amber-liquid courage was gone, replaced by choices determined by appearance and whimsy. The effect was immediate. I found myself holding forth to a group explaining the significance of my upcoming 21st birthday and what it meant in America. I was numerically a man. I could vote and assume privileges and responsibilities I was only vaguely aware of. I remember their smiles that kindly humored my sophomoric enthusiasm. I then found myself involved in discussion of *My Fair Lady* with a young actress who seemed to enjoy my commentary and insights. When she was leaving I felt compelled to walk her out to her taxi and gushingly compliment her boyfriend on his good fortune. I then joined a group discussing classical music and in voicing everyone's favorite work. I knew a few composers' names and individual pieces of music, but could not assign one to the other. I moved on.

My final memory was of sitting on a couch with the most attractive of the two women I had seen in the kitchen. Her name was Eleni, and she was a fashion designer from Greece. To my amazement she was laughing at everything I had to say, though I remember nothing of what I said. When she excused herself to call a cab I gallantly volunteered to do it for her, then looked for someone to explain how to call a cab. I walked her out and asked to see her home. She said: "If you like." I got in and was in foreign territory as to what to do next.

The taxi stopped minutes later in front of her flat, and I asked if I could call the next day. She said: "If you like." I asked for her phone number and, after much fumbling, found something to write on. She told the driver to return me to my place of origin. Not able to contain my excitement, I burst into the remnants of the party and announced I had her phone number. After puzzled looks I made it across the hall and crashed.

The next morning I painfully attempted to sort out the events of the previous evening. What was fact and what was hallucination? Who was real and who was fantasy? The phone number? Where was the damn phone number? Rick and I spent the next hour looking for proof of what happened the previous evening. Finally, my shot record! Her phone number was scribbled on the one document protected above all others. It was a record of all the shots we had received from day one of our enlistment. There were no backup records. Lose it and you were subject to starting over. I rushed to the nearest payphone and dialed and immediately hung up, realizing I didn't know what to say or how to say it. Where was the support of Johnnie Walker when he was really needed? I finally worked up the courage, dialed and heard the voice I had dreamed about. "Is this Eleni?" She affirmed it was, and I asked if she remembered me from the previous evening. She affirmed she remembered me. I asked if I could see her that afternoon, and after a long pause she said, "If you like."

We set a time and I returned to our flat grinning like the Barons Court cat. I showered, put on my most sophisticated outfit, got Rick's approval, and headed to foreign and frightening territory. Her name was listed in the directory of the apartment building indicating she lived on the third floor. There was only one Eleni. I rang and heard a window open directly above and saw her lean out of the window and ask if I would go to the pub around the corner and get a pack of cigarettes. She threw down a key and said it would get me in the front door and to come up when I returned. On my way back I saw a street vendor and bought roses, hoping that's what men did in this situation. I knocked on her door and was greeted with a smile and an embrace. She suggested I might be more comfortable if I removed my trench coat and sport coat.

When we left her flat that first afternoon she gently took my elbow and guided me curbside, explaining that a gentleman is always outside of the lady when walking on the sidewalk. A not-so-gentle etiquette lesson took place the first time I took her to dinner. I was very hungry and finished my dinner in record time and, looking up with a satisfied smile, I saw a look that would have stopped Odysseus mid-voyage, followed by a command to never do that again. Ignorant of what I had done she quietly explained that food was to be enjoyed, not merely consumed, and leaving her with a full plate while I sat across from her with nothing in front of me was an insult to her and the restaurant, and a sure sign I was not ready to mix in civilized society. Weeks later she prepared and explained how to eat a continental multi-course meal.

On our fourth weekend I could tell there might be a problem. Eleni wasn't sure our being together was a good idea. She was concerned about our age difference. She had made up her mind each of the past three weeks to tell me it had to end but changed her mind each time. That was the last it was discussed, except when we planned a long weekend at a seaside resort and weren't sure whether our May-December relationship would be the scandal of the weekend. It was a different time.

Our time was from Saturday night to early Monday morning. We referred to our time as "Only on Sunday," in contrast to the 1960 acclaimed Greek film, *Never on Sunday*, starring Melina Mercouri, and featuring a soundtrack that won an Academy Award for best original song. Coincidentally, Eleni knew Melina from having been raised in Athens in an upper-class family, and from the fact her younger sister was an actress in Greek films. That was the extent of her history shared with me, except the mention she had been married to a British naval officer. I never knew the status of their relationship - married, divorced, or separated? Eleni was a very young woman when the Nazis occupied Greece. I asked her about the experience, and she said it was a terrible time and would possibly talk about it when we knew each other better. She never did.

I brought little maturity and virtually no sophistication to our relationship. I realized, from Eleni's perspective, I was a project, but we grew into our relationship.

On Sunday mornings we explored neighborhood markets, mixing the practical with the social. Our favorite was Notting Hill, and the weekly ritual established a comfortable domestic intimacy. In bad weather, Sundays involved a film, usually a British *New Wave*, or foreign film I didn't understand, with subtitles I had never seen. There rarely was physical action, only men and women navigating the complex avenues of love and loss. They were never in color and rarely had happy endings.

The movies were followed by dinners at different restaurants where I learned how and what to order, dining etiquette, and basic wine selection. I was introduced to international relations, politics, and history from a Greek perspective. I also was learning the art of casual conversation, requiring awareness, informed opinions, genuine interest in your partner, and gentle humor. Summer afternoons were spent at gardens and museums, enjoying London's vast and varied opportunities, and each other's company. I was a fast learner. I had a great teacher.

The schedule worked for both of us. Eleni had a Monday-Saturday life she needed for her professional and personal commitments. I would have been hard to explain. We played out what introducing me to friends and family would be like. We always came to the same conclusion. No. My weekend life gave me two London evenings and one full day for my entertainment venues and museums and galleries. We didn't discuss Sundays until Saturday night.

A year after we met Eleni was thinking of returning to Greece. Her father was ill, and she missed Athens, family, and friends. She knew I was returning to America in six months and thought this might be a good time to return to a country she hadn't lived in for ten years. Her hesitation concerned social restrictions that a single woman from an upper-class Athenian family would face. The government was in constant turmoil, and she was used to being free from social and political constraints.

Eleni was mature enough to know we had no long-term future. I do not know the depth of her feelings for me, but know whatever it was deepened over time. We avoided the issue until she said she was leaving for Athens in two weeks. I managed a brave front. I wanted to thank her for her kindness, affection, and patience. Her influence crushed my insecurity and ignorance. It is easy to dismiss my feelings as the result of first love, but that is dismissing love as a singular entity, not as the complex integration of multiple emotions and experiences. In hindsight I marvel at how little we knew about each other. We never took pictures and rarely asked questions. What was volunteered was at the initiative of the other. Our life together was contained in our brief history. Maybe it was because we always knew it would end soon.

A few months after Eleni left for Greece I received an "early out," which changed my discharge date from November to July so I could begin college. Two months into the semester found me doing well academically and admired as a veteran and sought after by the opposite sex, intrigued by my absence of the sophomoric behavior of many of their former high school classmates. Vietnam was becoming a daily headline. The draft was still in effect. I had served. I was the most relaxed man on campus. My problem: though the young women were bright and attractive, I found it impossible to find a level ground of interests and experience. I missed the importance and satisfaction of my old job, I missed London, and I missed Eleni. They couldn't compete.

One day I came home from school and found a forwarded postcard buried at the bottom of a pile of mail. It had a brief message: "Eric, I am back in London. Here is my new address and phone number. Call me. Eleni." My initial response was to pack and grab a plane. Reality then took hold: "And then what?" After a few sleepless nights my pattern of indecisive actions prevailed. I did nothing.

To my ever-lasting gratitude, my future brother-in-law, Stu, arranged a 1964 New Year's blind date with a former high school classmate. Her name was Patricia Gebhardt. She was attractive, had a warm and spontaneous smile that could not be faked, and an infectious laugh that welcomed those first met into her presence. My attraction to her was immediate and life-lasting. She also had good sense, insisting we meet prior to the official blind date, and if I passed muster, insisting we not be alone, that we celebrate in a group that included Stu and my sister, Judy. From that humble beginning, Pat Gebhardt eventually became my life-partner, fully supporting my quixotic dreams and varied destinations. We now acknowledge New Year's Eve 1965 as our first anniversary, as important as our official June 22, 1969.

But it was not the idyllic course of true love. When we first met I was firmly in my developmental phase of bachelorhood, entertaining no commitments, still attempting to make up for my solitary adolescence. We were together for two years, and Pat finally determined that if I was not her future she was going away to college and seek her own. I encouraged her, a decision that lasted one semester when I asked her to return to Florida from Illinois in time for my graduation. It was important for her to be there. I wanted her to share that significant event. She was already that much a part of me.

I had graduated with my B.A. in English from Florida Atlantic University in Boca Raton, FL, in 1967, with no idea what to do with it. Education never crossed my mind, so I chose to become an airline pilot, based on the fact my father had been one and my older brother was following in his footsteps. The determining factors for me were that the career paid well and the time off generous. What I overlooked was they were passionate aviators, and I was a sightseer by nature.

I had accumulated almost fifty hours of flying time and was ready to take my Private Pilot's exam. I needed to practice the maneuvers I knew I would be tested on but hadn't performed for quite a while. I flew west to the Everglades and climbed to 2,000 feet and cleared the area. I began practicing stalls. After my third try I knew I was doing something wrong: the plane would shudder and go into a slow and shallow dive. I vowed to give it one more attempt and, after putting the nose on the horizon, realized my oversight. I was forgetting to reduce the throttle as I raised the nose. The plane went into a violent dive. I pushed and pulled every pedal and stick available and found myself heading straight toward a herd of cattle that were getting larger every second. I pulled out of the dive at 500 feet, due to no skill of my own, attempted to regain my composure, and headed back to the field. I parked the plane, never to return.

Following graduation I had read an article in *Esquire* magazine, written by a San Francisco State University professor, who made San Francisco sound like a city unmatched by any other in America. I had proposed marriage to Pat but indicated I needed one more expedition before settling down. I had to go to San Francisco. I saw an ad in the paper looking for someone to drive a car from Ft. Lauderdale to San Mateo, CA, just south of *The City*. A week later we tearfully parted, her father wrote off my promise of marriage and, in November 1967, I headed 3,000 miles west. I was also praying I still had the luxury of Pat's faith in me, deserved or not.

My faith held. She allowed me to change career directions with no visible potential for success. She eventually joined me in San Francisco, and we officially began our lives together on June 22, 1968. She would be a wife and mother who put everyone else first. She was always there, and while waiting for me, discovered her career niche. She had worked as a secretary but returned to college to become an elementary school teacher, discovering her passion and natural talents, and becoming the kindergarten teacher parents want for their child's initial exposure to formal education.

Pat made one demand of me once both careers were underway. I had to promise to visit her Kindergarten class at least once during the year. My fear came from my first visit when I prepared a lesson on careers, and what five-year-olds would need to study. I hadn't prepared for future professional wrestlers and dinosaur trackers. A few years later I dropped in unexpectedly, wanting to surprise Pat and fulfill my promise for that year. I walked in and saw the students all drawing boats with their crayons. Pat turned, smiled, and asked the students for their attention. "Children, I want you to stop what you are doing. We have a guest who is very important to me. Does anyone want to guess who it is?" After a time of focused stares, one boy finally raised his hand. "Is he Christopher Columbus?" The boats being colored were the *Nina*, the *Pinta*, and the *Santa Maria*. I had walked in on Columbus Day. My fears were well founded.

We often saw her students on weekend ventures to the supermarket. That is where I met the "flying five-year-old" who, upon seeing his/her teacher, screams, yells her name, and gets a running start down the aisle and tackles her around the knees. I also met many "incredulous kindergartners" who, upon seeing their teacher, suddenly realize she is a mere mortal who also requires sustenance and paper products.

I am aware that many adults still remember the name of their Kindergarten teacher but have a problem with grades beyond that. Her name was Mrs. Seaton, and seventy-four years later I remember exactly what she looked like. She was beautiful.

I had never written a love poem, but due to another challenge by Chanel, a Valentine's Day contest requiring a love poem of twenty lines or less that could win an all-expenses-paid trip to Paris for two, I gave it a try. Pat encouraged me to do my best. I didn't win anything, but at least I got my love poem out of the way.

MEASURES OF LOVE

The heroic, tedious battle to conquer time fades as I
Measure my life by moments you have touched.

Mechanical measures fail to match your scent that invades my day:
    The hidden memory of your taste and smell
    Springs unsynchronized surprises on my senses,
    Reminding me during pedestrian moments
    Of the when and where of you.
Celestial movements seem random to your perfectly timed caress:
    In the haze of fitful sleep
    My blind fingers scramble across the bed,
    Desperately seeking the silk of skin or gown,
    Ending my search in the cradle of your warm body.
Historical epochs pass unnoticed against a lifetime of private rituals:
    A knowing glance
    Sifted through a crowd of weaving bodies,
    Promising shared insights, laughter,
    And practiced passion.

As granules measure the quantity of our lives,
Shared moments build the memories that tell us we have lived.

***

I grew up in the 1950s. The domestic model was men as breadwinners and women as homemakers who, if they had to work did so at an entry level, with little chance for professional advancement. During my four years in the military the only women I encountered were nurses. In my five corporate years with *United Air Lines* in San Francisco in the late 1960s and early 70s I never encountered any women who were considered for the management training program. Their point of access was to become reservationists or stewardesses, with restrictions on age, weight, and marital status. When I started my community college career in the mid-1970s I encountered women who were department chairs, deans, vice presidents, and presidents. With the rapid growth of community colleges across the country the numbers of women in administration continued to grow, though I remember being asked when I interviewed for my first administrative position – "Would I have a problem working for a woman?"

In 2009, and into my fifth year as president of the newest Alamo college, I read an article in *The Chronicle of Higher Education* that discussed the status of the "Glass Ceiling" in higher education. Not too positive at the university level but much better at two-year colleges. That afternoon I had my leadership meeting consisting of Directors, Deans, and Vice Presidents – eight in all. To my amazement all were women. I shared my discovery with the staff. They weren't surprised. They knew they were women. I began to worry about the imbalance, but also knew they had come through the hiring process as the best candidates. I comforted myself by knowing we had men at the department head level who were showing great potential for future leadership.

7. INFLUENCES and INFLUENCERS

I am a product of all I have read, seen, heard, experienced, and all who have crossed my path during the past seventy-nine years. My responsibility has been to sort the quality and embrace the value. I am neither the puppet nor the puppeteer, but rather the being responsible for shaping and sharing who I have become. The arts transported me beyond the radius of my senses. I chose my friends and mentors well. I idolized no one, but respected and learned from many.

THREE WISE MEN

1. Rick Busch: When I finally settled into my daily routine at RAF Chicksands and learned my responsibilities I fell into favor with three colleagues who would become best friends and mentors: Rick, Fitz, and Bill. Rick, Fitz, and I shared a room in the newly finished dorm – leaving our WWII Quonset Hut for newbies to follow. Rick was five years older and from upstate NY and the person who convinced me to start taking the University of Maryland classes from professors who would come in from London every week. I'm not sure I would have begun my higher education career without his insistence that I was college material. Because of his support I accumulated a year's worth of college credits by the time I finished my tour. I also had the eye-opening experience of taking Freshman Comp using Hemingway's *A Farewell to Arms* as our text, and learning a different American History as taught by an Englishman who explained the reason most Brits were ignorant of the War of 1812 is because they were busy fighting a fellow named Napoleon.

2. Frank Fitzpatrick:

February 3, 2018

Dear Pat and Family:

I was so saddened to hear of Fitz's sudden passing. I know there will be many who will share wonderful stories about this special person, and I want you all to know how much his friendship meant to me and how important his influence was in helping me grow into adulthood. We shared a room and a bed for two years. I had the upper bunk and Fitz had the lower. We also shared our past lives and future hopes and dreams. Fitz and Rick Busch were surrogate big brothers: both were a few years older and had been to college. I was not certain if I was college material. The three of us worked different shifts, and contrary to many of our peers, took advantage of our proximity to London. We would each come back from our London trips and recommend activities we had discovered – plays, concerts, museums, historical sites. They helped me realize how unbelievably lucky we were to be in one of the great cities of the world, and why we should take advantage of our good fortune.

Pat, this was before he ever met you. I remember distinctly one day in 1963 when Fitz came back from London and announced he was madly in love with a beautiful red-haired actress he had seen in a play titled, *Mary, Mary*. That actress was Maggie Smith, one of the greats and most recently of *Downton Abbey* fame. Obviously, his good taste never left him.

For two years I threatened to accompany him on one of his early morning runs. I never did but wished I had. I also remember the single object he kept on his nightstand for the two years we roomed together: a complete set of Lawrence Durrell's, *The Alexandria Quartet*. He vowed to finish it before he left England, but I'm not sure he ever did. Four years later I did finish all four books and wanted to thank him for the great tip.

And finally, just a note on how we saw our futures. I wanted to be the next James Bond, but Fitz would say that what he wanted in life was a good job and a wonderful family. How successful he became.

You and your family are in our hearts and prayers, and Fitz is forever in my wonderful memories, with eternal gratitude.

Eric and Pat Reno

3. Bill Lawrence: When I was introduced to the internet in the mid-1990s I was also introduced to the internet white pages. I could look up anyone I wanted with a few strokes of the keys. Who had I lost track of, who did I remember most prominently, and why? Bill Lawrence was the first name that came to mind. I hadn't seen or communicated with him since 1964 when I was discharged from the Air Force,

Bill was an old guy when we first met. He was twenty-one. We were in awe of him, for special reasons. He thought and didn't speak until he had something of value to say. When he did speak, everyone stopped what they were doing and listened. We had skull sessions, just as college students have in their dorms. I loved to participate and was rather full of myself. I could argue three sides of the same issue with equal passion. After one session, when we were walking back to our dorm, Bill put his arm around my shoulder and said: "Eric, will you do me a favor?" I assured him I would. "Don't ever talk to me again unless you know what the hell you are talking about." It must have had an impact because I have never forgotten.

I typed in his name and the city he was from, Charleston, South Carolina. Four names popped up, and I vowed to call the four numbers over the holidays. Two nights later our phone rang and my son, Patrick, answered and said: "Dad, it's for you. It's a Bill Lawrence." After thirty years we both had decided to reconnect within two days of each other. I told him why I wanted to contact him, but he didn't remember having said anything memorable and thanked me anyway. We got caught up, talked about Rick and Fitz, and vowed to set up a reunion as soon as possible. It took two years, when I had a meeting in Washington D.C. Rick lived in D. C., having retired from the CIA, and Fitz lived in Philadelphia, having retired from the Social Security Administration, and was probably the only SSA employee fluent in Russian. We convened at Rick's and picked up where we left off thirty years before. It was a magical evening, and we vowed to do it again soon. Six months later Bill passed away from stomach cancer. The remaining three kept in touch and saw each other periodically. Fitz died in 2018, but Rick and I see each other every time I am in D.C. and communicate regularly.

Bill Lawrence's influence just kept on giving. Fear, a liability if it limits or restricts, but beneficial if it guides and challenges. I never realized how much I personally and professional benefitted from being afraid of rejection or failure, and how much it was interpreted as being thoughtful and reflective. I learned to let the world reveal itself in any new situation before committing myself to it.

When I returned to America and started college I was surprised at how often I was told by student colleagues how much I was admired. I was seen as "deep." I was able to trace the origin of their praise to the fact I was a few years older than most, and I didn't speak unless I had something to say. They assumed I was thinking in the silent times. There is also a mathematical component to holding back, listening more than talking, being confident that what you are about to share will provide benefit. Most serious discussions begin on a broad base, followed by the generalities of the chaff, finishing with the substance of the wheat. If you wait, the work has been done and you can provide additional substance. You are the new and fresh voice. You are "deep."

When I reached England I worked with many colleagues who had been to college and were continuing their informal education by reading the *Times,* the *Guardian,* the *Stars and Stripes,* and current bestsellers. My bunkmate, Fitz, had two years at Penn and had just finished a year at the U. of Indiana learning Russian. I had to catch up!

Many in the dorms were members of book clubs. The two most popular were the Literary Guild and the Book of the Month Club. I chose the Literary Guild because it sounded more sophisticated, its depth of title. Those who joined were entitled to a gift: the not to be missed offer of a set of the *History of Western Philosophy.* I was hoping to take my adolescent brain to a place it had never been. My Guild gift finally arrived, having divided all of philosophy into two volumes, secured in a beautiful case, and weighing in at approximately twenty pounds. For a full month I faithfully chose a volume and spent one hour each night getting frightfully intelligent.

At the end of the month I decided to step back a few volumes and start my intellectual growth with popular fiction. I was truly fortunate in discovering Ian Fleming's *James Bond* series, being read by seemingly everyone on base and a year prior to the first Bond movie. We also were fortunate to have two of the seminal American novels of the 20th Century published during our USAF years: *To Kill a Mockingbird* and *Catch-22*. They were books we all read, traded, and discussed. Those three years were littered with the blessings and glue of common experiences.

We can never anticipate the source of our positive influences. They can be literary and artistic giants, internationally known historical figures, Nobel Prize winners, or they can be the neighbor next door.

Feb. 18, 2010: REMEMBERING DENNIS O'SHEA

Dennis O'Shea was a neighbor and headed the Fort Lauderdale FBI office. Most of the kids on the block had fathers who were loved and admired, but Mr. O'Shea was a G-Man! He looked like what we imaged a G-Man should look like – tall and straight. We didn't know what he did but knew it was important and possibly dangerous. According to his obituary, when he took over the FBI office he simply told the media: "They [the mob] will know we're around."

Decades later we learned he was born in Manhattan and by age eighteen was with Patton in France, providing relief to Allied troops during the Battle of the Bulge. Prior to his passing he was awarded France's highest honor, the French Foreign Legion Medal of Honor. Two years after WWII he was playing basketball on the National Champion Holy Cross team, featuring future Boston Celtic and NBA Hall-of-Famer, Bob Cousy. In 1959 he brought Cousy to our house so I could meet him, but I was nowhere to be found.

On occasion I was asked to baby-sit their young son and was surprised by the interest Mr. O'Shea took in my schooling and outside interests. I told him I loved basketball and baseball and hoped to play for the high school. He told me he played basketball in college and suggested we meet at the local court. After a half-hour it must have been obvious to him that basketball was not my game. But he offered encouragement, tips, and future lessons.

Knowing of my interest in baseball he suggested I read the classic sport's novel, *Bang the Drum Slowly*, by Mark Harris, later made into an early Robert De Niro movie. He gave me his copy and we talked about the story when I returned the book. It was my first literary exposure outside of a classroom – an experience not of our household. After I graduated from high school he arranged for me to interview for a job testing concrete samples for construction sites – a job I'm sure he was aware would accelerate my decision to go to college or join the military.

Dennis O'Shea was a model of what it meant to be a father, professional, and patriot. When I hear assaults on the integrity of our intelligence agencies I think of all the Dennis O'Sheas and their unselfish commitment to our democratic ideals. They were the heart of the "Greatest Generation," becoming institutional and personal models for all who followed.

Eric Reno

MID-POINT PHOTOS

1. Dad's early aircraft: Waco 10 – 1938

2. Dad's aircraft with Mom as passenger – 1938

3. *TWA* Capt. Max Eugene Reno – 1941: "To the best 'Mom' there is. Capt. Max Reno"

4. Betty Jane Reno – 1941

5. Dad and Grandma Reno – 1942

6. *TWA* Skycap and friend of Dad's – 1942: "To Max Reno, one of the best Pilots I know. From Sid"

7. Dad and "Rick" – 1956

8. Last family photo, taken the evening prior to leaving for Air Force Basic Training – November 1960
Back Row: Alan and Eric (Rick)
Middle: Judy, Mom, Dad
Bottom: Tim, Scott

9. First UK home (Quonset Hut) – February 1962

10. First day in the UK – 1962

11. Tech School classmates and life-long friends:
Eric, Hank Harrell, Bill Wooton – Spring 1962

12. Chicksands roommates: Top – Eric and Frank Holly, Bottom – Frank Fitzpatrick and Rick Busch – 1962-64

13. Most influential mentor: Bill Lawrence – 1963

14. Our Man in Paris – 1963

8. The SECOND HALF

What have we learned? How have we lived?

My four years following high school and completion of military service was the period where I began to grow, leaving behind adolescence, and discovering who I might become. This compressed and colorful period of life experience was all I could have hoped for. I handled the opportunities with enthusiasm and managed to learn and apply the lessons that presented themselves. I saw the world, encountered guides, overcame my social ignorance, renewed my faith in my academic and intellectual abilities, and met my life partner. The future was confusing, but no longer daunting, yet there was still "miles to go" before becoming an educator.

In the Fall of 1972 Pat and I were expecting our first child, though not at the best of economic or professional times to be starting a family. I had turned thirty and had left corporate life in San Francisco to return to Ft. Lauderdale and family, where I hoped to begin my career teaching English at a junior/community college. I had not been a competitive commodity in San Francisco. I now had a M.A. in English but no teaching experience. I knocked on doors at my alma mater, Broward Junior

College, tried Palm Beach Junior College, and Miami-Dade Junior College. Nothing.

Of my visits, the one to Palm Beach Junior College (PBJC) was, though unsuccessful, the most inspiring. I was told I should see Dr. Watson B. Duncan III, a legend at PBJC and throughout the state and beyond. Burt Reynolds credited Dr. Duncan with being his inspiration for his interest in the dramatic arts, and the performing arts facility bears the name, the Duncan Theater. His name was intimidating enough, but I was desperate. I arrived late one afternoon, found his office, saw the open door, and knocked. He was as I imagined: white-haired, distinguished looking, with theater and literary memorabilia everywhere. I introduced myself and asked if he needed part-time English teachers. Before answering my question he offered me a chair and began asking me about myself – my background, my experience, my goals, and my passion for teaching. I had nothing to offer: no experience or concrete goals, other than getting a job. He didn't have anything for me but advised me to keep asking, if that was truly what I wanted to do. I was about to leave, but he had a story to share with me.

One day a student came by and said he wanted to thank Dr. Duncan for saving his life. The young man had been in one of his classes but dropped out and joined the army during the Korean War. He was caught in a firefight between his line and the enemy's. Bullets were whizzing overhead, and he dared not move. The horrific and endless time had him considering whether to stand up and get it over with. Then, a poem

Dr. Duncan had asked them to memorize occurred to him, and he spent the hours until dark going over it, the meaning finally becoming clear. "I wanted to thank you for saving my life."

Dr. Duncan wished me well and told me teaching was a wonderful profession, but I would never really know the effect my efforts had on my students. But do your best, show your passion, and make it meaningful to your students. I asked if he had seen the student again. He said he hadn't but did go to the Registrar's office and had them change the young man's grade from an "F" to an "A."

I was beginning to panic. I faced the Catch-22: we can't hire you because you have no experience. Get experience and we will give you a chance. The Friday before the semester began I again stopped at the newest campus of Broward to see if teaching opportunities had become available. I had interviewed months before and was questioned by the Department and Division Chairs, both retired military, as to whether the Governor of Ohio was right in bringing the National Guard onto campus at Kent State. My teaching abilities were never explored. The fact my most recent degree came from San Francisco State University, a prominent reference in the current annals of student rebellion, may have had something to do with the subject of my interview.

It was late afternoon and the parking lot almost empty. I saw the door of the English Chair's office open and stuck my head in to ask about any openings, and before I could say a word he said: "I have three sections that made today, and I need a teacher. Are you available?" My career had begun: 8-9am, 9-10am, and 10-11am, MWF (Monday, Wednesday, and Friday). All three classes were Freshman Composition. He gave me the texts and said he would see me on Monday. I had a whole weekend to decide what I was going to do for the 45 hours of class time for each course. All I had hoped for in establishing a new career was in my lap. The only thing I needed to do in the next two days was figure out what and how to teach.

When I got home I learned I had received a call from Marymount College in Boca Raton, wondering if I was available to teach two classes on Tuesday and Thursday. Same class, different texts. Over the next fifteen weeks I managed to survive and learn, by trial and error, how to be a teacher. I learned it was best to be organized and consistent. I thought my youth and recent experiences in San Francisco would enthrall my students, and we would have deep philosophical discussions, resulting in publishable essays we would all share. I left twenty minutes open for discussion on that first day of class. I wondered if that would be enough. I started the discussion and waited for comments. Not a hand. It was one of the longest twenty-minute segments of my professional life, but it was the beginning.

There were days early in my teaching career when I wanted to track down students from my first-year classes – and apologize for my less-than-outstanding performance. When Pat and her mother were away visiting friends and family in Illinois I spent two days in bed mid-term of my first semester, convinced I had chosen the wrong profession, and not knowing what to do next with my life and the responsibilities of a first child and an uncertain future. When I returned to the classroom I realized I must be doing something right: there were students who were engaged, responding to assessment, presentation and discussion. They were my touchstones of confidence. Elizabeth (then Karyn) Snead was the type of student that teachers cherish. She was bright, radiant, and wrote like the professional she would become. Her involved and responsive presence, and those of students like her, helped keep me afloat that first year.

Fifteen years later we found ourselves working across the street from each other in downtown Fort Lauderdale. I was the VP for Academic Affairs at Broward Community College, and Elizabeth was the Fashion Editor for the *Fort Lauderdale News Sun- Sentinel.* We caught up on lives and had lunch periodically. She introduced me to sushi and to John de Groot, a kindred Hemingway spirit who had written an award-winning play titled, *Papa.* Elizabeth soon left and became everything show biz, featured in *People* magazine, *USA Today, Hollywood Reporter, L. A. Times,* and *E-Fashion Police* – not to mention the multiple venues and outlets she created or represented. Her talent and success were obvious during those first courses of my unsteady professional beginning. This is a belated and heart-felt thank you, for her and all those students who supported and taught me to teach at the very beginning.

* * *

Pat and I had decided on natural childbirth, the current trend, attending classes together and preparing our partnership for our new family. My students were aware that our first was scheduled to arrive the week of final exams. They became members of our support group, receiving updates and marking the calendar. The time had arrived, Monday, December 11, 1972. Pat entered the hospital with regular labor pains. I called Broward and Marymount to let them know I wouldn't be in the next day. They wished us well and would put us in their prayers. I was with Pat for the next six hours and was advised I would need to leave, not something that was part of the natural childbirth classes we had taken. I would be brought back when the baby had been delivered.

What I had expected to be a short time drifted into hours. The doctor had been napping, waiting for the time to deliver. Four hours from the time I left the delivery room something was happening. New people showed up, moving in and out of the delivery wing quickly, passing me with strained smiles and downward looks. Finally, at 6:00am, I was told the baby had a suppressed umbilical cord, depriving him of oxygen. They could not tell if he would survive, and if so in what condition. Thirty-two minutes later Matthew Blake Reno passed away. Pat's survival was still in question. An hour later she had been stabilized but had received significant damage that would take months to heal. She was not given medical clearance to conceive again for eight years.

I faced returning to my mother-in-law's house and our bedroom we had decorated to double as a nursery. Her mother and I didn't know what to say to each other, no words that would have helped. After a fitful sleep I returned to the hospital to sit with Pat and attempt to provide love and comfort at a time most needed for both of us. The next day I began the effort of meeting with my five classes during their final exam period. I vowed to be a tower of strength and explain and answer questions as to what took place. The word had spread quickly from the time I had contacted the department chairs. Their faces reflected their concern. My tower of strength crumbled at unexpected moments, with many joining my physical grief.

We faced the pain, replayed every step we wished we could have changed, attempted to avoid the assignment of blame, and cried separately and together. Thankfully we were surrounded by family and friends and managed the holidays. The hardest challenge was being surrounded by friends and family and their beautiful children who represented what we had lost. With every child were humorous instances, unique achievements, stories foreshadowing great promise, and the multiple opportunities for parental involvement. We put on our strongest faces, often finding excuses to leave gatherings early. We were the silent and wounded, within thirty minutes of sharing the great and trivial moments of Matthew Blake Reno. We were advised to seek counseling. I said I would if they could assure me our tragedy never happened. Pat said she felt the same way, our decision determined by our conviction there was nothing to be said that could ease the pain and erase the memory.

The death of our first born changed our plans for making Florida our home. I had successfully completed my first semester of teaching and was anxious to dramatically improve on my heartfelt, yet artless performance. I improved my second semester and was offered a full-time position at Marymount but had my heart set on teaching at the junior college. Nothing was available. That summer we had one free pass left on United Air Lines and flew to our first home, San Francisco, hoping the trip might help to heal. We drove to the wine country and passed Sonoma Valley High School. I turned the car around, parked in front of the school, went into the office, and asked if they had an opening for an English teacher. They made a call and sent me into town for an interview with the Superintendent and High School Principal. I was offered a full-time position and the opportunity to be Junior Varsity Baseball Coach. I loved the community and the students and was in line to work part time at one of the local wineries, something I learned that many in public education did on weekends and during the summer.

We thought that returning to northern California, a place of great memories and happiness, would help in our collective recovery. But as the semester progressed Pat was in visible need of the support of family and friends. The place and its history were not enough. In desperation I met with the school principal and tearfully requested to break my contract so I could get Pat back to home and family. He granted my request and wished us well. I shared my decision with my students who listened silently, appreciative they had heard it from me.

When I left Florida for Sonoma I had thanked Dr. Shelby Lee, the new Broward North Campus English Department Head, for considering me for any positions that might become available. He said he had heard good things about my teaching and would keep me in mind. I dropped him a note that I was returning to Florida and would like to teach part-time again. A week later I got a letter from Dr. Lee telling me they had a fulltime position beginning in the Spring. January 1974 began my forty-year career in community college education. We were blessed professionally and personally at one of the most crucial times in our lives. Dr. Lee became a friend, a mentor, and a savior.

9. FAMILY: Phase II

2022: A PRAYER for the UNWANTED CHILD

I pray that all children have someone who:

1. Holds them tight when they are afraid.
2. Protects them when they are threatened.
3. Soothes and cares for them when they are hurt.
4. Feeds them when they are hungry.
5. Clothes them when they are cold.
6. Applauds them for every accomplishment.
7. Laughs at their innocent antics.
8. Teaches them when they are curious.

I am pro-life, but not the term with multiple and ever-changing definitions used in politics and religion to divide our country. My pro-life is limited to the formative lives of children not yet completely influenced by the morals and manners of those responsible for their welfare. Children love without question, trust without reason, respond without cause. They do not hate, nor do they discriminate. They are consumers of attention and praise. They are the greatest responsibility we have as individuals and as a society.

The abuse of that sacred responsibility is what troubles me most. The horrors visited upon the innocent are daily occurrences that challenge our ability to imagine, but also take place in our presence. We have seen children who are raised by the yell and disciplined by the hand. But there is also lasting damage to those who are neglected and ignored.

Damage to the innocent takes many forms: the physical, emotional, psychological, and the seemingly benign. I must borrow an iconic line of dialogue from Arthur Miller's play, *Death of a Salesman*, where Willy Loman's wife demands that her husband's life amounts to more than what little he accomplished: "Attention, attention must be finally paid to such a person." That same passionate appeal surely applies to the helpless innocents who are brought into the world. Life itself guarantees none of what they need and deserve. That is left to us.

We all have incidents in our lives that, for whatever reason, never leave. I have two that surface whenever I see children who deserve better. I was on the Board of the *Childcare Connection* of Broward County, FL, whose role was the education and certification of childcare facilities and programs. Part of my orientation was to visit a variety of sites. One visit was to a program in a public housing community.

We were joined by residents, and I was closely followed by a young boy of approximately four or five years of age. He was without an adult and would position himself next to me at every stop. I returned his attention, but he never smiled or responded and stood as stiff as a toy soldier. At one stop I thought he might want to see a point of interest. I stooped to pick him up. His body froze and he stared at me, fearful of what might come next. He didn't know how to be held. I set him down, expecting him to run away, but he stayed close. When we were leaving he followed me as far as he could. I knelt to say goodbye and attempted a hug. His body stiffened, his eyes following me until I was out of sight. I do not know what created his fear of contact and silent desire for closeness.

Anything would be conjecture, but I feared that the life a child deserves was not his experience.

Pat and I were having breakfast at a popular restaurant in San Antonio when a young mother and daughter (age eight or nine) were seated two tables away, and directly in my line of sight. For the next forty-five minutes I watched the mother order food and spend the remaining time eating and scanning her cellphone, never once communicating with or looking at her daughter. The girl never attempted to address her mother. She sat with a practiced silence, knowing her role. I know how minor this example is compared to horrific others, but I cannot forget that morning and the girl, quietly sad beyond her years. "Attention must be paid!"

Family of origin. Do we replicate, borrow, or avoid the patterns of behavior we inherited from the families that gave us life? Will I be my father, in piece or whole, or a new creation? The easy answers: I will not smoke; I will not drink to embarrassment; I will be involved in my children's activities to the extent possible; I will support their interests and opportunities financially and emotionally; I will talk to my children about what I think and feel, and ask them to do the same; I will do everything in my power to make them feel safe and secure as they grow and develop.

At age thirty-seven we become a two-income family. Pat got a job as a Kindergarten teacher, and we were able to afford our first house, something I thought would never happen. The GI Bill allowed us to purchase a $50,000 home, even though we qualified for only a $48,000 loan. We signed a promissory note to pay $50.00 a month under the table for the remaining $2,000. We affectionately labeled our first abode the "snake house." The previous owners had planted a large cactus under each window, an environmentally friendly security system. I destroyed five large shovels making our house less safe. Our backyard bordered an elementary school and its playground. I wasn't aware that on moonlit nights the basketball courts would be used 24/7. The last remodel was removing large pieces of plywood that had been stacked in the corner of the backyard. As I removed the last sheet I discovered a nest of large snakes that had made the area their home. For how long I wasn't sure. What kind they were and to where they scattered are questions I never asked nor wanted to know.

Nine years following the death of our first born, Patrick Matthew Reno was born on Pat's birthday. It was one of the most anticipated deliveries among family and friends. Everyone knew our history and our fears. I was poised to start the phone tree contacts. A large, collective sigh of relief. Patrick was healthy and beautiful and Pat was doing well, but we were advised this should be her last pregnancy.

April 1992: **OUR NOT SO UNTROUBLED CHILDHOODS**

As a not-so-young child of the sixties and early seventies, I am occasionally amazed, via hindsight, at some of the naiveté that helped form the way we viewed the world we were about to remake. One that has occurred to me since the birth of our son six years ago was the belief that if we could somehow recapture the innocent and carefree world of our childhood, then we could reform a world founded on adult corruption. This attempt to transpose the beauty and innocence of childhood was reflected in the music, the poetry, and the games we played – and yes, by the ideas and solutions we proposed.

Almost twenty years have passed since the power of the flower and the discovery that the world is a bit more complex than we had realized and that being an adult did have some advantages. When Patrick was born in 1981 he was very special to us for a couple of reasons: he was our first child who had lived (a son Matthew died eight years before at birth), and he came during what is considered late in life for his parents. For those reasons I am presumptuous in believing that we have attached more than the usual significance and attention to everything he did and everything that happened to him.

Anything that indicated a threat to his innocent world received the same hovering scrutiny with which we listened to every breath during his first weeks of life. We discovered that he had fears that we, as adults, had no way of anticipating or protecting against. They were unique to someone encountering phenomena for the first time, with no experiences upon which to construct protective barriers and rationalizations. When Patrick was almost four years old he was afraid to go to sleep because he was sure of having nightmares. We made the mistake of lying down with him until he went to sleep. It was a mistake in terms of precedent, but it was also the time our most interesting discussions took place. The fear of night and darkness produced a "secret way of sleeping," with both hands clutched around the right leg – a sure method for preventing bad dreams. One evening we were determined to make Patrick go to sleep by himself and heard the tearful reply to our suggestion that Pooh Bear would be sufficient company: "A bear isn't real; I want to hold something real."

Death was a topic that surfaced in a variety of forms; initially with the surety that our Thanksgiving turkey would be going to "turkey heaven," to the natural concern about what was going to become of Mom and Dad. Patrick wanted to know how old he would be when I died and informed me that I couldn't die until he had grown up. We also discovered how careful we must be in explaining adult fears to children.

We were paranoid about the possibilities of kidnapping and child molesters and did all the right things in discussing the issues with Patrick: we talked about the difference between good and bad people, strangers, codes, etc. One evening, long after our last talk on the topic, Patrick asked if we would miss him when the bad people took him away. This example, more than any other, made us aware there is no way we can predict how young minds process the information they receive. A less heartrending example that made the same point is the time he asked me: "Dad, you know when I grow up to be a big man and go to work? What do I do when I get there?" I dare any adult to list that as a potential concern they could have predicted from any child.

As Patrick began school we saw his world filled with worries and concerns related to impressing his peers. I watched him repeat the Pledge of Allegiance in his sleep so that it would be perfect for the next day's class. I was puzzled by his reluctance to buy his school lunch, something he had always looked forward to doing – until his mother relayed how he had seen a classmate, with a full tray of food, trip and fall in the cafeteria, which resulted in laughter from the whole room.

These examples of youthful fears are obviously not earth shattering or unique to our son. Every day we read of children who have faced unbelievable physical and psychological horrors, and I cannot begin to know what fears fill their dreams. But it is an adult opinion that places Patrick's fears in the "un-earth-shattering" category. I doubt if he would agree with that assessment. Childhood can and should be a special time in our lives, filled with the awe of growth and discovery. But it has never been carefree – no matter what adults may have remembered or wanted it to be.

We expanded our family late in life. We were in our mid-forties. We visited the Children's Home Society and asked about adoption. We were told we were older than usually considered as adoptive parents. But the more we talked the stronger the possibility we were being considered. The next week we received a call and were asked if we would consider twins. We had never considered that possibility but said we would. A few days later we met the fourteen-month-old Amanda and Alaina. The foster care mother indicated the twins were the first of over eighty previous foster children they had considered for permanent custody. At our first gathering to meet Amanda and Alaina, the thirteen-year-old boy who had shared a room with the twins for the past six months stared daggers. We were taking away his almost sisters.

The initial transition went smoothly except when Pat was out of sight. Amanda and Alaina were inconsolable until she returned. We each had to lie next to a crib and hold the hand of one of our new daughters until they went to sleep. This lasted for a few weeks. Her friends arranged a shower for our new daughters three days after we were awarded custody, at a home forty miles away. They told Pat she needed to be there at 2:00pm. The twins napped until 3:00pm. I told Pat that Patrick and I would get them dressed and drive to the shower. They were fine when they awoke, but when Pat was nowhere to be seen, the hysteria began. Patrick's job was to sit between the twins' car seats and entertain and distract them for the length of the hour's drive. He deserved the highest medal that can be bestowed upon an eight-year-old civilian. They screamed up to the front door of the house but ceased immediately when they saw Pat. The ran to her and had a great time the rest of the afternoon eating sweets and mixing with the fawning gathering. Patrick and I found the punch bowl and a place where we could restore our hearing and our nerves.

We fell in love with our beautiful daughters and became a family of five. Of course, identical twins would have to be 180 degrees different, but it would be hard to imagine our lives without the joy they have brought us. They've had themselves as company and exhibited the traits of twins: a secretive language, imaginary friends, and coincidental behaviors. Watching the behavior of twins is a fascinating pastime. It never gets old.

As with all adoptive parents we faced the question of when and how to tell. Theories and recommendations were plentiful, and all had merit. There were stories of both successful and difficult transitions. We chose to wait too long, under the theory the older they were, the more maturity they would bring to the news. There never seemed to be a good time – the issues of appropriate age, the uncertain physical and psychological forces of puberty and adolescence, and the guilt of having withheld the information into adulthood. There were also the long periods when we forgot. They were our daughters and always had been. The distinctions of origin didn't matter. Physical traits in our family are very strong. Amanda and Alaina had none of those. We were fortunate our decision-making wasn't held against us, but am also sure there were feelings they did not share.

Our three children were not part of our early lives. They were never part of the economic and professional struggles. Their father had always been a college administrator and their mother, an elementary school teacher. We had close family and wonderful friends. We lived 200 miles south of Orlando and had an annual Florida family resident pass to Disney World that we used at the spur of the moment. Our children never referred to the resort by name. It was always Mickey's House.

We attempted to balance love, discipline, support, and guidance. Our impact on the growth of our children into adulthood will never be determined. Ours was more directive, while our relationship with our parents was passive, never expecting anything beyond their role of being parents. We now watch with interest our children's relationships with our grandchildren. We all do it differently, but always with love. Patrick, the English teacher, was always a good student, popular, and athletic. He is the "intentional educator," more structured and scholarly than his father – a perfect teacher for the rigorous International Baccalaureate (IB) program found in many high schools. He had intended to go into the field of Sports Management.

In 2002, after his first year at his home university, Colorado State University, he went online and managed to get an unpaid internship with the PR Director of the Fayetteville (North Carolina) Patriots, one of the teams in the fledgling NBA (National Basketball Association) Developmental League. He used his year's tuition to rent an apartment and gained professional and social experiences beyond any expectation.

His boss, office colleagues, and the players were primarily African American. He became the official scorer for the team and had to earn the respect of the players, for whom statistics were the objective measure of their value. He asked his boss why he was chosen for the position, a nineteen-year-old student with no experience in PR. "I liked your interest, and you were the only applicant who didn't want $75,000 to do the job." Patrick also loved being a minority, learning what was not taught about professional sports, and learning from basketball legends who were in and out of the organization. It was an education no money could have bought.

From that internship Patrick walked into high-level graduate student positions at flagship universities in Oregon, Kansas, and Nebraska. When asked where Patrick went to college I am proud to detail the stamped academic passport that reflects his travels: he was a *Ram*, a *Patriot*, a *Duck*, a *Jayhawk*, and a *Husker*, not counting the mascot for Maynooth, the National University of Ireland, where he spent a semester abroad. But maybe his greatest accomplishment was marrying the beautiful and talented Nancy (Nurse Practitioner and teacher), and growing a family with three wonderful grandchildren.

Amanda and Alaina are physically identical, but with reputations of being Miss "Neat Freak" and Miss "Disarray." In addition to being beautiful, they are strong. They were founding members of the cheerleading squad of a new high school and were "bases," those who held up, tossed, and caught. No one worked harder, exhibiting elements of character that have stayed with them as they have grown into adulthood. They were a revelation to watch.

Amanda is our RN and MD to be. She is structured and organized, and expects others to be the same way. She is a brilliant writer but has no interest in recreational reading. Amanda worked at Outback Steakhouse when she was in high school and added another seven years beyond that. She was one of the best they had at any job level, and we waited for her to decide what to do with her gifts.

When I was in Texas I received a call from Amanda asking, "Dad, guess where I just came from? The community college!" I matched her excitement and asked if she knew what she wanted to study. "I want to be a nurse." She had never expressed interest in the medical field. I congratulated her and got out of her way. She whizzed through with top grades, comprehension, and application, with only one misstep. She called in tears and was sure she was going to get her first "B." She didn't and finished with an "A." We are just waiting for her to decide her next academic advancement.

Alaina is our Medical Assistant and Aesthetician, rescuer of dogs and lost souls. If given the opportunity she would build a shelter for neglected and unwanted animals – especially dogs, especially beagles. She is as smart as her sister, but not as driven. She knows all things concerning beauty treatments and offers advice to her mother and father, welcomed or not. She has difficulty understanding why life isn't fair. Like her sister she has the potential for succeeding in anything she undertakes. We are just waiting for her to discover her niche, while also raising a beautiful granddaughter. Watching Alaina grow in maturity as a single parent has been a joy to watch. Having the responsibility for the welfare of another person has become the most important role of her life. She has responded beautifully.

We have been blessed with bright and big-hearted children and four beautiful grandchildren, but that doesn't stop us from being excessive worriers. I expect most parents who have lost a child would be in that category. When Patrick was going through adolescence I never slept until I heard the garage door opening. Why? I was once an adolescent male. On the other hand, the same rule applied when our daughters were of that age. Why? Because I was once an adolescent male.

Every parent has the right to worry about the challenges of adolescence. I share this baseball-related cautionary tale about adolescent behavior. In the summer of 1956, our father flew the Brooklyn Dodgers Triple-A baseball team, the Montreal Royals, to their away games. In September he flew the parent club, the 1955 World Champion Brooklyn Dodgers. Their championship was the first in the history of the storied Dodger franchise. When the regular season ended he brought a gift for me (14) and brother Alan (16): an autographed baseball of the 1955 World Championship team. We thanked him, read the names, and decided to play catch.

We couldn't find a ball so decided to use the new one. Within a half hour no evidence of autographs was visible. Years later I looked up the roster of the Champs, cross-referenced with members of the Baseball Hall of Fame (HOF), and discovered we had played catch and destroyed a ball with signatures of eight members of the Baseball Hall of Fame: Jackie Robinson, Roy Campanella, Pee Wee Reese, Duke Snider, Sandy Koufax, Don Drysdale, Manager Walter Alston, and Dick Williams (inducted later as a manager). First baseman Gil Hodges was announced as a member of the HOF Class of 2022. Make that nine members, as the tragedy grows.

Forty years later I told a friend who was a baseball card and memorabilia collector, and asked what he thought a mint condition autographed baseball of the 1955 World Champion Dodgers would be worth. I thought I saw moist eyes, knowing more than he was sharing. Why did we do it? We were adolescents, and why parents fear that stage of development. Anticipating consequences is not a strength.

10. The POWER of PLACE

It was always the going, never the leaving.

New living locations, and their timing, force the acceleration and development of social and interpersonal skills like no other event, not counting tragedies. As an adult I have benefitted from every place lived and every position held. I have met good people everywhere and gained experiences that have enriched and fashioned my life. I have thrived as a "stranger in strange lands." But for the first time, because of pen to paper, I wonder if I was also in search of something I had lost.

1942	Allegan, Michigan & Chicago, Illinois
1942-1954	Mission/Overland Park, Kansas
1954-1960	Ft. Lauderdale, Florida
1960	San Antonio, Texas (Lackland Air Force Base)
1961	San Angelo, TX (Goodfellow AFB)
1962-1964	Shefford/London, England (RAF Chicksands)
1964-1967	Ft. Lauderdale
1967-1972	San Francisco, California
1972-1973	Ft. Lauderdale

1973	Sonoma, California
1974-1992	Ft. Lauderdale
1992-1998	Fort Collins, Colorado
1998-2004	Lakewood/Denver
2004-2014	San Antonio
2014-present	Fort Collins

Three Years in Another Town: London/UK

They were *Blokes* and we were *Yanks.* "Ta" was "Thank You," French fries were chips, potato chips were crisps, fish and chips replaced hamburgers, pubs replaced bars, bitter replaced beer, MGs replaced Chevys, the right lane was traded for the left, and the girl back home was replaced by a beautiful young lady with a delightful accent. The anglicization of young Americans was a natural result of a three-year assignment to the UK. We were young and at the beginning of our adult lives.

Tom Brokaw eloquently labeled WWII adult Americans as the "Greatest Generation" because of their courage, sacrifices, and accomplishments during that global conflict. The label is well deserved, and the young Americans who came to the UK in the early 1960s were joining a society that was almost solely responsible for saving western civilization as we then knew it. For those who doubt, read the accounts of how France was transformed during their four years of Nazi occupation. The depth and breadth of their sacrifices were still visible and felt those fifteen years later. Only the war had changed. It was difficult to find any English family that did not have some familial connection to the United States. When I first traveled the Tube, black and white images of the stations serving as bedrooms of the Blitz surfaced in my memory.

Many Americans re-enlisted at the end of their four-year tour, with the goal of a military career and the incentive to extend their stay at Chicksands, plus the $450.00 re-enlistment bonus for the additional four years of service. For those who received other assignments, many had the goal of getting back to Chicksands ASAP. It is fascinating to Google the Chicksands' social sites and read the commentary of many who had served, and to get the sense their three-year tour was one of the highlights of their lives. The later veterans included female airmen who seemed to be in equal numbers to their male colleagues.

I have wanted to thank someone for my three years in England – a time responsible for all that followed. I have drafted Letters-to-the-Editor to *The Times, The Telegraph, The Observer,* and the *Guardian*. None were sent. This is probably my last chance. My assignment was the reverse transport of the 17th Century Pilgrims. I had a new old world to discover. It wasn't just a foreign land; it was also a foreign time. It was the London I wanted it to be. I was challenged by responsibilities beyond any I could have imagined and provided a cultural and historical setting far beyond anything I could have designed. It was a quantum leap from a life of relative safety and limited exposure, to the outliers of acceptable behavior, imagined experiences and adventures, and meaningful relationships.

London wasn't a city. Given my lack of any cosmopolitan experience, London was a continent. It had its own countries and villages, and native populations speaking an almost foreign language – all providing unlimited opportunities for discovery. I was on a train to London almost every Friday after work. I preferred to travel alone, unencumbered should adventure present itself. I loved going to places on a whim, choosing entertainment venues last minute, never worrying about arrangements or compromises. There was one constant possession that accompanied me on my weekly journey, my secular Bible, *The A-Z Street Atlas of London.* It got me to and out of my uncertain destinations, providing a comfortable assurance that nowhere was off-limits or out of reach.

I was usually joined at the Friday night bus by African American airmen, including teammates from the baseball team. They were going to the "Smoke." They knew where they were going and who they were going to see. For many, London was the first major city where they didn't have to be concerned with blatant discrimination. There were neighborhoods where they were welcomed, especially by citizens of the far-reaching Commonwealth, particularly those from Africa and the Caribbean. When we met on the return train it was obvious they had a wonderful time, and would be returning the next week. I would love to have joined them.

There were remnants of the Blitz. In the winter the fog was thick, and the air was dirty. It would take until Wednesday for coal traces to stop showing in my handkerchief. It was Holmesian and Dickensian. I wandered London streets and neighborhoods into the night, never sure where I was going or how far I was from my hotel, and not sure if I could find a cab at that hour. I loved the city's historical beauty and the magic of those hours. On one of my late-night wanderings, the elements I hoped for were in place: cold, overcast, slight fog, just enough moonlight to see structures in the distance, and unknown neighborhoods. I came around a corner and saw I was near the Thames, with Parliament in the distance, and a ribbon of cloud drifting across the face of Big Ben. I stood and looked in every direction for a long time, then followed the river to where I knew I could find a taxi. Imagination and fantasy realized.

Every weekend I usually made a pilgrimage to Foyle's Bookstore on Charing Cross Road, overwhelmed by what I hadn't read and what I didn't know. I kept a list of reading material that had been recommended or was curious about. For a person who had never seen a play I landed in the middle of the golden age of stage musicals: *Blitz, My Fair Lady, The Sound of Music, Pickwick, Oh! What a Lovely War, Camelot,* and *Oliver.* I was convinced by my roommates to buy a subscription to the National Theater, under the direction of Sir Laurence Olivier, with performances at the newly constructed Royal Festival Hall. Every performance included names, if not internationally known, would be over the next four decades. I was close to musicians whose albums I was collecting, having a seat that looked over the shoulder of Milt Jackson, brilliant vibraphonist of the Modern Jazz Quartet (MJQ). I had never been exposed to live performances of any form, but soon took it for granted. It was as natural as going to a movie back home. I was fortunate to be able to start at the top.

I loved more than London. The lush green countryside was populated by quaint villages, centuries-old architecture and structures, and vaguely known location names. The bus from Chicksands to Bedford always stopped at RAF Cardington, which had housed the training for crews and the manufacture of barrage balloons designed as a defense against low-flying German aircraft. That stop, and the view of massive hangers, was a constant reminder that WWII was not ancient history.

But what had the greatest impact on my cultural transformation was the trains. My introduction began at the kingdoms of King's Cross (est. 1852) and St. Pancras (est. 1868), both sharing the same Tube stop. Both rife with Roman connections, none I learned or remembered, though King's Cross attained global celebrity as the departure station for young wizards traveling to Hogwarts.

My first trip to London introduced me to those stations that were coated with decades of smoke and soot – no glistening metal and glass. The places seen, the people met, the romance, plotting, treachery, and discovery they could share. They were my departure and arrival points on my weekly journey between Bedford and London. I never needed to make reservations, having to know only the first and last trains of the day.

In between it seemed there was a train leaving for my destination every hour.

On my second trip to London I searched destination names on the monster electronic schedule. Many I knew for their national and international prominence. Most I had never heard of. Pronunciations were a challenge. I shudder to think how often I asked directions to "Lychester" Square, finally being told by a nice gentleman, in a gentlemanly way, the word, "Leicester," was pronounced "lester." I took pride in cataloging corrected giveaway mispronunciations and inserting the corrected versions into conversations with English friends and acquaintances to show how much of their culture I had mastered.

Though I usually took the train into London, on occasion I enjoyed taking the milk-run bus that stopped at the end of the road to our base and made what seemed to be twenty stops until reaching London. I fantasized about getting off at each village to spend the day, finding surprises of history, and wondering who I might meet.

After three years in England I was ready to go home. I was homesick and ready to begin a vaguely conceived and frightening future. The closer I got to my separation date the more aware I became of my unbelievable opportunities and experiences, what I was leaving, and what I wished I had accomplished. I wondered if I would ever get back to the UK to see and do what was unseen and undone. My reverse homesickness hit hardest when I was given a ticket to watch *Trooping the Colour* (the Queen's annual birthday celebration) rehearsal the month before I left. The pomp and ceremony that was a part of our daily lives would be missed. It was going to be more of an adjustment than I had anticipated. Queen Elizabeth II was just completing her first decade as Sovereign when I arrived in 1962. For three years she was my honorary sovereign, and I was her honorary subject.

San Francisco

My time in San Francisco began six months after college graduation, with little or no thoughtful planning. After delivering a car in San Mateo I took an inventory of my current situation: no plan, little money, no transportation, no contacts, no employment. The first thing I needed was transportation. I found a 1955 Volkswagen for sale for $450. I took a bus to my first sight of the magical city. There was no magic in the neighborhood of the garage that had the car. The VW was painted Afrika Korps olive green and had a reserve fuel tank that was activated by the driver's foot once the main tank was empty. I paid half of my remaining cash and drove off in search of the city I had read about. I saw hills and headed to the top. I got behind a line of cars waiting for the light to change. Upon green they took off. I hit the gas and went nowhere. I had just discovered that a 1955 Volkswagen didn't have the power to reach the top of many of the hills from a standing uphill start. I waited for the cars behind to go around, backed down to the bottom of the intersection, and looked for smaller hills.

The next day I found a hill with a breathtaking vista of the Bay and the Golden Gate Bridge. I walked the neighborhood, seeing now why *The City* had gained its reputation, but when I returned to my car I saw a ticket under my windshield wiper: $40.00 for "not curbing my wheels." Having come from a place where the highest elevation barely exceeded sea level, I needed an explanation. I asked a passerby who kindly explained that "curbing of wheels" was protection against runaway automobiles on steep hills. My financial resources were fading fast.

I missed the 1967 "Summer of Love" by three months, but the counterculture was still in full swing. I went to Golden Gate Park and saw what I had missed that summer: more love, freedom, hair, and interesting clothing than was seen in Boca Raton in a decade. At Florida Atlantic a radical was a philosophy major. In San Francisco being a semi-hippie seemed to be the default.

I found temporary work in the Post Office for the Holidays and spent them in my studio apartment. It was the loneliest holiday season of my life, with only one person to blame. My Christmas dinner was the Blue Plate Special at the 24/7 diner. After the New Year I had an appointment near the airport with a company called IBM. I don't remember how I got the appointment or why I wanted it. I arrived early and killed time by walking into the adjoining office of United Airlines. I asked if they were hiring. They took my resume and ask me to have a seat. Ten minutes later they invited me into a conference room and said I had an appointment that afternoon at the administrative offices downtown. They were interviewing candidates for a new management training initiative, an eighteen-month program rotating candidates through different functions of the company. They were looking for the "well-rounded" individual. My liberal arts degree was perfect. Two years later they wouldn't have talked to me without an MBA. Was I interested? I jumped into my Afrika Korps transportation, headed north, interviewed, and was given a start date for the next week to begin orientation. Pat and I were married that June, and she got a job as a secretary at the United Airlines maintenance base near the airport.

San Francisco was the perfect place to spend the first four years of married life. We fell in love with the city: the people, the diversity, the beauty, the sophistication, the booming and rapidly changing culture. It was a four-year honeymoon, with the added benefit of airline perks – traveling the world first class free and staying at the best accommodations for fifty per cent off. Our first free passes came from *Air India* and took us to London. Pat was introduced to and would share a passion for my beloved London. London was our favored destination over the four-year period.

Between the two of us we had more free passes than we could use. On occasional weekends we would check the movies and menus of the First Class cabin of flights from San Francisco to the east coast. We would take a 9:00am flight to NYC or D.C. for a First Class lunch and a movie and take a return fight at 7:00pm for a First Class dinner and a different movie. I saw a bright future and couldn't wait until I was eligible to apply for the management program. I worked in the large travel center on the corner of Post and Powell, overlooking Union Square, learning the industry, and watching people get on and off the Powell St. Cable Car. The world entered our doors daily.

I was learning the business and given added responsibilities. At the same time I discovered a passion for sharing the literature I had read in college and the current literature I was discovering on my own. That was the beginning of my educational and professional journey. I began to see enough of corporate life to question whether it was my future. Pat remained supportive of my dilemma and let me decide which path to take. After being told by a well-intentioned colleague that I was going to lunch with the wrong people, my decision was made. I enrolled in the Masters in English program at San Francisco State University, just a few blocks from our garden apartment.

When I finished my degree I attempted to gain classroom experience, but everyone wanted to be in San Francisco, and I couldn't compete with those who had experience and a professional resume. Pat was expecting our first child in December 1972, so we decided to return to Florida, move in with my mother-in-law, and hope I could begin my new career. I was thirty years of age, with a growing family, no job, no home of our own, and no immediate prospects for a new beginning. I had more personal responsibilities with fewer prospects. I was frightened but could not admit it to those who had faith in my well-thought-out plan, and who were depending on me.

Florida

South Florida was the home of my adolescence, the achievement of becoming our family's first college graduate, and the home for the first eighteen years of my professional career. I was not a sun worshiper, nor was I interested in water activities. I preferred frost and fog over beach and burn. The temperature and humidity figures were hard to tell apart. The weather was too hot, humidity too high, roads too crowded, communities overbuilt, and a unique natural environment slowly being destroyed by unmanaged growth. However, our family, friends, and professional experiences and opportunities were unmatched.

For Pat, South Florida had everything: the ocean, sun and sand, our dream home (our first with a swimming pool), her career as an elementary school teacher and the friends that went with it, and family on both sides of our marriage. People moved to Florida for her reasons. If it had been her choice we would still be in Florida. Why then did I choose, at age fifty, to relocate 2,000 miles to the west, for a lateral administrative position, for less money, at an institution that had five per cent of the resources and facilities of Broward Community College, to a community I had never heard of?

I still cannot answer that question to anyone's satisfaction, including my own. There was no reason for leaving, only for going. Something was missing. I had to prove something to someone. I traded a secure future, in an enviable professional position, and put my family at risk. Pat was the most affected by the uprooting of our lives. She supported my decision but was losing much she wanted in life. Our children were eleven and four. We were separated for a year because of a slow real estate market, and she was left with the parenting and the day-to-day responsibilities, though I was in Florida for every birthday and every holiday, and Pat and the children came out to visit their new home. I had taken a calculated risk that produced sleepless nights.

Colorado

In addition to my vaguely stated reasons for uprooting our family, I saw Colorado as a quality-of-life move. Our children were young, we lived in our Florida dream house in a wonderful neighborhood, but we wouldn't let them out of the house unless we were there to watch them. The news always led with the latest random acts of violence and drug deals, and I became paranoid about their future and looked for someplace where they could have a childhood close to the one we had experienced. I applied for a CEO position at a community college campus that had been a vocational-technical school, located in Fort Collins, a town I had never heard of and whose population was 2,000 or 200,000, for all I knew. Denver, a major metropolitan city, was only fifty miles to the south, an area I would call home for my six final professional years in Colorado.

The contrasts in community life and geographic setting were 180 degrees from that of South Florida.

Fort Collins is located at the base of foothills that front the Rocky Mountains. The views were breathtaking, in contrast to our previous home, whose highest elevation was the sixteen feet of a highway overpass. It was a contained and defined community, versus the sprawl where community boundaries and governance were impossible to distinguish. The civic sense of community was refreshing, always with the purpose of making Fort Collins a better place to live.

The summer I arrived I volunteered for a community-wide initiative to address an ugly incident where a minority college student had been victim of a racial epithet. The Mayor, City Council, University President, School District Superintendent, and Chamber of Commerce organized task forces and committees to seek answers and design programs that would say loudly to the community: "This isn't who we are or want to be." It was a refreshing change. I had found the community I was looking for, and it wasn't long before I started seeing Fort Collins on the national lists of "Best Places to Live, Raise Children, Retire, Do Business."

I wanted our family to be seen as community assets. Patrick entered 6th Grade and loved his new school, made friends, was popular, and involved in academic and athletic activities. The college was two miles away. One day I got a phone call from Pat that she had received a call from Patrick's school, letting her know he had been sent to the office for rude behavior to his teacher, Mrs. Johnson. I drove to the school and asked if they would get him out of class. We stood outside and had a heart-to-heart, and I reminded him his mother and father were teachers and expected respect from their students. He agreed, vowed it would never happen again and would apologize, and returned to class. We saw Mrs. Johnson a few weeks later, and she told us she had never seen a parent do that during her teaching career and thanked me. Two miles was not far away.

San Antonio

San Antonio was the last stop on my professional journey. I had come full circle. On November 9, 1960, I landed in San Antonio to begin Air Force Basic Training. During training we were allowed one day to explore the city. We took our shaved heads, our heavy horse blanket overcoats, were driven into town and dropped off in front of the Alamo. We were told the bus would return at 8:00pm, and we had better be there. We were given one piece of advice: "There are lots of things to see, but whatever you do, don't go near the river." There had been attacks against airmen at different parts of the river. The River Walk is now one of the main attractions for residents, visitors, and shaved-headed recruits. That's how long I had been away.

I returned for the first time in March 2004 when I interviewed for the position of "Founding President" of a soon-to-be-built community college in the Alamo Community College District. I had missed the many national conventions and conferences scheduled in San Antonio. Everyone seemed to have a good time in San Antonio. I didn't know what to expect.

I knew of the rich Hispanic heritage of the area and looked forward to being a minority. San Antonio is a city of traditions and celebrations. It was easy to believe what a fourth-generation resident once told me, that San Antonio is the favorite Texas city of most Texans. I was quick to discover the Hill Country to the north and the German and Alsatian pioneers that founded those communities. There was a connection. My great grandfather had immigrated at the age of sixteen from Alsace-Lorraine, though he never made it to Texas.

San Antonio is a city that attracts visitors. During my ten-year residence my older brother, Alan, and his wife, Fran, came to visit annually from Kansas. We toured the city and surrounding countryside. Creating a home-cooked meal was *verboten*. There were too many new restaurants to try and too many favorites to return to. Fran is a strict Catholic and never misses Sunday Mass. We would surprise her by taking her to a different church, many with historical roots that would even attract the non-practicing Renos to join her.

The military culture that permeates the area, once known as "Military City USA," revived the memories of my four-year tenure and renewed my pride in my abilities and performance. The location of the college is northeast San Antonio, heading towards Austin, and a few miles from Randolph Air Force Base, once dubbed "West Point of the Air." Toward the city is historic Fort Sam Houston, the home of the beginning of military aviation, and which housed the Brooke Army Medical Center, the destination for many of the most severely wounded soldiers from the Middle East, and in SW San Antonio is Lackland AFB, still the destination for recruits going through basic training.

The cultural influence of the military included active, dependents, and retired. Randolph AFB is home to the Air Education and Training Command (AETC), which is responsible for all AF training, including the Air Force Academy. There were valuable lessons in education. We marveled at the skills and attitudes of many who were not considered college material. High expectations, structured learning, and the practical application of what was learned, produced confident professionals who guarded the health and safety of our nation. I shouldn't have been too surprised. I could have looked in the mirror. The military also provided the college with wonderful employees and serious students. No excuses, just performance.

AETC was under the command of a Four-Star General, the closest the United States will come to having royalty. I was asked to become a member of the Citizens' Advisory Committee comprised of civilian leaders. We had annual three-day trips to different training centers across the country, usually in a C-130. We were invited into the cockpit, crawled on our stomachs to see and be within 100 feet of a mid-air refueling demonstration, had lunch at the Air Force Academy with graduating cadets, fired a range of weapons, and watched the training of the Air Force version of Navy Seals. A few of our group were retired military. I took great pride in assuming I was the lowest ranking of those with a previous military history. Not bad for a three striper.

In addition to those perks I become the Honorary Commander of the 435th Fighter Training Squadron, located at Randolph, under the welcoming leadership of Col. Bruce Smith. The 435th trained the fighter trainers. My honorary designation produced the highlight of Pat's time in San Antonio. The 435th convened a family gathering of trainers, spouses, and children every Friday afternoon at 4:35pm on the flight line, two hundred feet from the T-38 Talon trainers, the latest in the distinguished family of military aviation education. We were invited and looked forward to every Friday afternoon, and fell in love with the family dynamics of those who defend and protect. Pride is a weak description.

Pat was invited to participate in the "Spouse Taxi" event that brought the spouses to the base for a day to be teamed with a trainer. They were oriented, briefed, suited for flight, introduced to the history and technology of the aircraft, ending with being taxied to the end of the runway. Pat's movie star handsome pilot/trainer, Tony, was charming and patient. The only instruction Pat remembers him giving was: "Pat, whatever you do – don't touch anything." She almost didn't participate, believing she would be too nervous and much older than the other participants. She had a memorable experience. At the end of the day she heard one of the young spouses ask how the little lady did? A few years later I took twelve of the photos and created a calendar of the event. Pat hung the calendar on the most prominent wall of the kitchen, and if left to her, would have been a permanent fixture. The missing years and confusing dates would have been incidental.

11. The COMMUNITY COLLEGE

When I was ready it was there to welcome me.

Community/junior colleges are key to the strong foundation required for the maintenance and growth of a vibrant democracy. They are the educational vehicles offering social, educational, and economic mobility and equality. They are the affordable open door, flexible and close enough to provide educational access for every citizen, at any time.

When I graduated from high school in 1960 it was announced that a junior college would be opening in the old WWII Naval Air Station, located at the Fort Lauderdale airport, that until that time had served as a junior high school. Even though I wasn't ready for college there was no way I would start college at WWII facilities that once held students from a rival junior high.

In the 1960s, community/junior colleges were opening all over the country, fulfilling the promise of the Truman Commission of 1947 that proposed a community college within commuting distance of every American. Many experts cite 1960 as the beginning of the modern-day community college movement.

Between 1960 and 1975, on average, a community college campus was opening somewhere in the United States every week.

Community colleges also became the institutions that produced the majority of nurses, police, firefighters, IT techs, and many existing careers and those surfacing within the economy. Many of us brought an inferiority complex to the campus, but we also changed the national profile of who was entering higher education in America. We were the second wave to rock the selectivity of higher education access, following in the footsteps of WWII veterans using the GI Bill. We were: traditional, non-traditional, first generation, older, financially challenged, part-time, late bloomers, second and third chancers, minorities, majority female, and those who could have gone to any college or university in the nation. The American Association of Community and Junior Colleges (AACJC) lists distinguished alums on its website that are leaders in all areas of society: education, science, medicine, technology, business, media, the arts, professional sports, the military, and politics.

When I was discharged from the Air Force in 1964, the Junior College of Broward County, Florida, was my only option and had just opened permanent facilities the year before. In the early years many wanted to be seen as "little colleges" and prove the rigor was as tough, if not more so, than four-year colleges and universities. Broward was no different. It had a great library from the beginning, including a multi-edition reference collection of western philosophy – in German. It had excellent faculty whose role was to teach. Research was not an expectation.

As a student I was always in need of financial resources. The Viet Nam-era GI Bill didn't go into effect until 1966. I made it into the eligibility category by one week. If I had been discharged eight days earlier I would have missed out on thirty-six months of financial support, which paid for the last year of my bachelors, my masters, and half of my doctorate. That initial $100.00 per month was a life saver.

During my first semester I asked if the college had a baseball team. My advisor thought they did, and that I should go to the gymnasium to find out for sure. I was told to see the head of Student Activities and Athletics. He affirmed they had a team, and this would be their second season. I asked if they offered scholarships. They did, and I asked how I could apply. He asked what position I played. "I pitch." Was I any good? I told him I was. I got a $100.00 scholarship. I thanked him and walked out thinking: "We are going to have a very bad team."

When I was enrolling for the Spring 1965 semester I went from table to table seeking available cards for required degree courses that didn't conflict with baseball. I managed to get a schedule and presented it to the coach, who substituted my courses with Typing I, Basic Math, Pre-College English, Physical Education, and Health. He was intent on making sure his players remained eligible for the coming season. I spent the next hours secretly reversing his selections. But it didn't matter. I got to play, met good people, and began acclimating again to South Florida.

Over the next few decades the terminology of "junior college" began to disappear from signage and letterheads, to be replaced by "community college," a more accurate and welcoming descriptor. By the beginning of the 21st Century fifty per cent of entering freshmen into higher education and a significant percentage of college and university upper division and graduate students had begun their higher education careers at one of America's 1,200 two-year institutions.

***

Community colleges would often get delegations of educators from around the world who came to investigate the American system. They were impressed by the opening of access to all and the facilities that exceeded many of their universities. Many believed a version of our system could easily be replicated in their countries. But when they found out that community college students could transfer to major colleges and universities, public and private, at any time in their lives, they realized the issue they faced. Most representatives said their national higher education systems would never allow transfers from lesser institutions. University students qualified early, and the resources were reserved for those who had shown promise at an early age.

Despite the tremendous success of the community college movement, their international status and educational purpose have been diminished over the past two decades. I am disheartened as two-year colleges across the country have added selected baccalaureate programs and removed "community" and "junior" from their names. Being a community college once meant something, especially to those who believed they were welcomed for that second opportunity, and for those who never believed they were qualified to attend in the first place. I know there are many who disagree with my feelings, but the storied histories of those institutions that revolutionized educational access and success will fade as the generations pass. We will be left with colleges whose names communicate nothing of significance.

March 9, 2012: **COUNTING STUDENTS WHO COUNT or STUDENTS WORTH COUNTING**

I was a panel member for an article in the ***Chronicle of Higher Education*** (March 9, 2012) that focused on the flaws of local, state, and national accountability measures as applied to two-year colleges. The article dealt with two neglected areas: the lack of any recognition of students outside of the accountability database. Most national accountability measures include ONLY Fulltime and First-Time-in-College Students [FTIC]), and the complete neglect of that hard-to-measure element of teaching excellence. The accountability steamroller flattens any attempts to provide a meaningful exploration of institutional mission and individual student circumstance,

I would like to focus on a significant percentage of two-year students: 1) those who did not begin college as fulltime students, and 2) those who began as fulltime students, failed or stopped out, and returned to successfully complete their goals. It is these students who truly represent the special role two-year colleges play in building the economic strength and civic engagement vital to our nation's existence, and it is these students who are missing from the national dialogue concerning higher education accountability.

Understanding #1: Two-year colleges are NOT little universities. Their effectiveness should not be measured in the way universities are measured. Let's compare enrollments in public higher education for Fall 2009 according to the **NATIONAL CENTER FOR EDUCATION STATISTICS (NCES):**

	Four-year Public	Two-year Public
Total Enrollments	7,709,197	7,101,445
Part-time Status	27%	59%
Ages 25-65	31%	40%

The goal of a university student is to complete the baccalaureate degree, while the range of educational goals of two-year students would fill the first page of any college application. Given many current accountability measures, the following students would be counted as institutional FAILURES or not counted at all:

- First-time-in-college students who fail/drop out and return later to achieve a doctorate and a Nobel Prize.
- Any students who do not begin their college career as fulltime students.
- Students who take longer than three years to complete their two-year degrees.
- Active military, whose educational goals are stalled due to an assignment in Afghanistan (or any deployment).
- Students who get a job, due to having received skills from the partial completion of their program of study.

- Students who transfer to any private or out-of-state institution, without having completed a degree, and where tracking processes are not in place.
- Students who decide to "stop-out" for reasons too numerous to list, and who remain in good academic standing at their institution.

Understanding #2: One of the most compelling reasons for having a national two-year college system is to provide access to higher education for anyone, at any time. The single most unrealistic expectation we have for high school students is thinking they are ready for higher education upon graduation. We do not need data for this conclusion; a million anecdotes to which each of us could contribute should suffice.

Those who have taught in a community college know that one of the great attractions of the profession is the anticipation of seeing who will show up in our classroom. The dynamic of having recent high school graduates and students old enough to be their parents, in the same classroom, is something all teachers should experience. An added, and rewarding element of learning takes place as theory, practice, maturity, and experience intersect.

As educators and public decision makers we need to start being more deliberate in how and what we measure – given that the results will color public perception; determine public and legislative support; and mandate operational change. As public institutions it is our job to be accountable; it is also our job to ensure those measures are meaningful. There is too much meaningful work that needs to be accomplished to do otherwise.

Dr. Eric Reno, Founding President
Northeast Lakeview College

***

When I began my full-time professional career at Broward Community College in 1974, I was almost thirty-two years old, had found my calling, and considered myself the luckiest man on the face of the earth. My future was easy to predict: thirty years of teaching and then retirement, the reward for a job well done. I was in one of the best places at the best of times. Florida's twenty-seven-member community college system was a national model. Along with growth came opportunities. I had been a student at the original campus of Broward, got my first teaching position at the second and newest campus, became a founding division Chair at the birth of the third campus, became CEO of the first and largest campus where I began as a student twenty years earlier, and served a stint as the district-wide Vice President for Academic Affairs. I was well prepared for what professionally followed.

During my first academic year I was asked by our new dean, Dr. Roy Church, to co-chair a taskforce on designing learning labs. He asked me to send a memo to members announcing our schedule and first agenda. I asked my Department Head to show me the format for a memo. A few years later Dr. Church became Provost/CEO of the college's newest campus, the Judson A. Samuels (South) Campus, to be located on an active regional airport. He selected me as one of the three founding Division Chairs. One was a veteran, Dr. Nellie Dry, and Dr. Peggy Nash and I were fresh from the classroom. Dr. Dry mothered and mentored us, answering our questions, giving advice and encouragement.

Dr. Dry had the business and technical programs, I had communications and humanities. Dr. Nash supervised social and behavioral and physical sciences, and physical education. She was a good tennis player, but her knowledge of other sports was more limited. Our storefront wasn't ready for the beginning of the semester, and we had just a few weeks to schedule, hire, and find facilities. We found a church, close to our storefront under construction, willing to lease Sunday School classrooms. Every Monday we replaced elementary school chairs with rented folding chairs and tables, the process to be reversed every Friday afternoon.

Two issues remained: the screams of the church ladies when they went to the kitchen to prepare refreshments for a meeting, seeing enough dead casts for a sixteen-seat anatomy lab. The final issue was finding a site for Beginning Golf. The Friday prior to the beginning of classes Peggy burst into the room serving as everyone's office and announced she had found a golf course. Dr. Church's secretary, who was a golfer, asked: "Peggy, the Country Club is very selective. Do they know this is a class for beginners? What about the divots?" Peggy rose to her most imposing administrative height and said loudly: "If we need divots, we will order divots!"

Dr. Nash left after the first year, expecting her first child, and I was asked to take over her departments, in addition to the ones I had. I spent the next two years representing twelve departments whenever college-wide department meetings and issues took place that involved all three campuses. I was everywhere, loving every minute and establishing a presence and reputation. I also began to realize that I could do this. I had overestimated the competition. I had to drop the fear founded from an earlier time and follow the instincts that were standing me in good stead. My future mantra to returning students that living longer counts was applying to me. Dr. Roy Church provided me with opportunities and trust. I became a dean and campus CEO. He was a leader to emulate, and someone I never wanted to disappoint. He took his exemplary personal and professional skills to St. Petersburg, FL, and Ohio, leaving lasting legacies. We have remained friends.

I was almost a decade behind my professional peers. I had been doing other things outside of education: "exploring my potential" in the military and corporate life, and searching for where I fit. I admired the titled: Deans, Provosts, Vice Presidents, and marveled at their youth and grasp of global issues in higher education. Most would become presidents and beyond, and I paid attention to how they did their jobs, with never a thought I could follow in their footsteps.

I wasn't sure I wanted to continue the administrative path. I was a teacher. That is what I knew, loved, and did best. When the College got a new President in 1985, Dr. Willis Holcombe transferred me from the smallest campus (Provost/CEO) to the largest, and original campus. I accepted his decision with pride, though mixed with terror. It had 30,000 students, an aquatic complex, a Criminal Justice Institute, facilities and teams in intercollegiate athletics, a 1,200-seat performing arts center, a world-class planetarium, and many faculty and staff who were there when I was a student twenty years before. Dr. Holcombe modeled principled leadership and later became the Chancellor of the Florida system of community colleges. He provided me with the depth and breadth of experience, surpassing what many would experience at a stand-alone college. We have remained friends.

Within my first two weeks I was reminded that whatever path I chose, it required my full energy, attention, and commitment. I discovered earlier in the week we had a contract with the Broward Symphony Orchestra (BSO), and one of our music faculty was the conductor. Our performing arts center was a designated site for many of their concerts. One Sunday night I received a call from one of the Center's technicians. There was a big problem: the BSO had a concert, all 1,200 seats were filled, they had a guest conductor from California, and the percussionist had taken the wrong car and his instruments were in Boca Raton. What should they do? I covered the phone and silently asked: "How in the hell should I know?" I asked if there were spare instruments in the music building? There were, but they belonged to the faculty and were locked in an instrument locker. I told them to use those. They didn't have the keys and the faculty would have a fit if they found out someone had used their instruments. I said they had my permission and asked if they had a lock cutter. They did, the concert was a success, the faculty were quite upset. Problem solved. The staff had the answer but needed permission. I was in charge. It was my responsibility. Get used to it.

Another learned lesson was to stay within your depth of knowledge. Don't pretend to know what you don't. When I moved to the largest campus they were in the middle of an extensive and expensive updating of the planetarium. The college had received a large financial gift from the Buehler Trust that would fund a complete renovation of the dome, new furniture, a state-of-the-art Zeiss Star Machine, and the cost of bringing two Zeiss technicians from Germany to do the installation. Previously the planetarium was operated by faculty, but the new version would require professionals. After two months the technicians completed the installation and returned to Germany. The new Director and Assistant Director were fine-tuning the system. I saw Susan, the Assistant Director, in the cafeteria and joined her. "How goes the star machine?" "Oh Eric, it is beautiful. You must see it. We turned it on this morning, and the only problem we saw was Andromeda seemed a little bright." My star-gazing IQ begins and ends with the Big Dipper. I was never able to see the Little Dipper, Greek gods, animals, and all else.

On my way back to my office I decided to stop at the planetarium to see the new machine projecting on the new dome. The Director said: "Eric, you have got to see this. It's beautiful." He turned on the machine. It was beautiful, but I couldn't help myself. "David, it is breathtaking, but isn't Andromeda a little bright?" There was a pause. "Eric, that is an amazing observation, considering Andromeda is millions of light years away from this perspective." Let that be a lesson to you!

As I assumed administrative positions I did everything I could to demystify the position and humanize the holder. During my two final positions I began a ritual of participating in the first Halloween of my term. There was always a costume contest. At Red Rocks Community College I decided to dress up as Robin Hood, with the noble intent of robbing from the rich to give to the poor. I went through my son's collection of accumulated heroic paraphernalia and found a green hat with feather and a wooden sword. Pat contributed green panty hose. I contributed leather shoes from my San Francisco counter-culture period, green shorts, a wide belt, and a shirt with a laced front that must have been purchased from a Sherwood Forest department store.

I was a hit! Word spread that: "You have to see the President's costume!" The costume judging contest was usually held in the Student Center. A panel of student and faculty judges announced the winners: "The second-place winner is our President, Dr. Eric Reno, dressed as Peter Pan." I started to protest but decided to accept my award gracefully. In San Antonio the same confusion took place. I arrived in the morning as Robin Hood and exited the day as Peter Pan. I share this trivial story with what I hope is a serious observation. When you are in a leadership position it doesn't matter how you perceive yourself. It is how others perceive you that matters.

* * *

Broward Community College was one of the largest community colleges in the nation, with a reputation to match its programs and facilities. The Larimer Campus of Front Range Community College in Fort Collins, Colorado, could have fit its total physical plant into one of Broward's many classroom buildings. It was a former technical-vocational school built in the early 1970s. The facilities reflected the architectural philosophy that believed windows would distract students from their work. We assumed the facilities were designed by unemployed prison architects.

Though I was a vice president, I was the campus CEO. The Front Range President was located sixty miles south in a suburb of Denver. My job was to turn Larimer into a comprehensive community college campus. The challenges were the most satisfying part of the job. With dedicated employees, professional colleagues, and supportive civic partners, the campus was transformed architecturally and became an equal educational institution within the community, partnering on initiatives with the Poudre School District and Colorado State University. In five years, Larimer became the fastest growing community college campus in the State of Colorado and the site of the first community college and municipal (City of Fort Collins) joint-use library in the State. We proposed to call it the Harmony Library. One of the State governing board members thought the name a little too "touchy-feely." I pointed out the library was located on Harmony Road, one of the major east-west roads in the community.

After six satisfying years at Front Range I applied for a college presidency and was honored to have been successful. Red Rocks Community College (RRCC) is in a western suburb of Denver (Lakewood) and has an outstanding reputation due to its programs, employees, leadership, student achievement, and community support. I was succeeding a legend, Dr. Dorothy Horrell. She was now my boss, having become the President of the Colorado Community College system. I inherited a standard of leadership that was daunting, but Dr. Horrell was always there for encouragement and support. I became a walker, a talker, and a listener, visiting all areas of the college regularly, stopping by offices and meetings, learning about programs and people, and becoming a fixture in the community.

My initial fear was that I had moved beyond my abilities, my reach had exceeded my grasp. Fear was my co-pilot, but constructive fear is a great motivator. I surprised myself as I gained confidence and began looking forward to the social and professional events on a President's calendar and interacting with those recently met. Everyone has stories and all respond positively when I begin an introduction by asking to hear about their lives. They reciprocate and, along the way, our life stories intersect, and we have the beginning of a professional relationship and a potential friendship.

Asking for money. That was the part of the job as a college president where I felt most uncomfortable. RRCC has an outstanding Foundation Board, composed of members from across the spectrum of the community – most of whom had no personal association or experience with community colleges. When they learned the community college story and the community college students' stories, they were passionate and substantive in their foundation roles. My hesitancy was erased quickly by our Foundation Director, Ted Sandquist. After hearing my concerns, he stated simply: "Eric, if we don't ask them for money and support, someone else will."

Red Rocks was the only Colorado Community College to establish an Endowed Teaching Chair program that recognized excellence in the classroom in a significant way, including a three-year financial award and funds for the faculty member's professional development. The selected faculty member was chosen by the Foundation Board and offered in the name of the individual or corporate donor. This innovative program was patterned after that offered by my administrative alma mater, Broward Community College, who patterned theirs after that of Miami-Dade Community College. It pays to have been around.

Fundraising soon became one of my favorite activities. I looked forward to telling our story to all who would listen. Donors saw how far their gifts would go and were informed annually how they had been used, and who had benefitted. But my voice was secondary to those from the community who advocated on our behalf. One of the most rewarding events of the year was the Foundation Luncheon where scholarship recipients were seated at the tables of their donors, dramatically affirming the wisdom of their generosity.

My passion was working with students and ensuring they had every opportunity for personal, social, and academic success. I wanted them to always remember, with pride and a smile, their time at Red Rocks. I learned student leaders' names, attended and supported their activities and events, and let them know my door was always open. I was honored to be named *Colorado Community College President of the Year* in 2001 and 2004 by the State Student Advisory Council. No other awards or recognitions come close.

My favorite student organization was Phi Theta Kappa (PTK), the international honor society of two-year colleges. It is one of the most respected academic organizations in higher education. It promotes, celebrates, and recognizes institutional commitment to academic excellence. Their annual convention is attended by four-year institutions wanting to recruit PTK students, and offers programs and speakers featuring household names from every sector of the country, most of whom got their starts at two-year institutions. After I became a college president I was made an honorary member of PTK, which explains my lack of eligibility for earned membership. I knew how much work the College's PTK officers put into their responsibilities, and promised to fund their attendance at the annual convention to celebrate the year's work with 4,000 of their closest colleagues. I would also take the incoming officers to the convention so they would have a sense of what was expected of them for the coming year.

We held a pre-departure meeting, and I told them to hold a specific evening open. I wanted to host a dinner to thank them for their hard work and their role in promoting academic excellence at Red Rocks. We met in the hotel lobby and walked to the hotel's best restaurant. The great presentations, impressions of the 100 universities and colleges in attendance – and the scholarships being offered, dominated the conversations. Some students had never been on an airplane or out of state, and now they were being hosted at dinner by the College President!

The leather-bound menus were passed out, and I spent ten minutes silently watching reactions to choices and prices. Most were ready to order the chicken, the least-expensive item on the menu. Finally, I broke the silence and told them this was a "no liquor meal," but to pay no attention to prices. Order whatever they liked or have never tried, and to make sure to order an appetizer and a dessert. After a collective sigh, one of the most rewarding sessions of the trip for the President began. All were asking questions about selections, laughing about who was ordering what, "ohs and ahs" when the food was presented, sounds of approval when it was tasted or shared, and satisfied smiles around the table at the end of the meal. This event is not forgotten. Education comes in many forms. Not all require a grade.

One day I received a call from our Director of Student Life. He said a group of students wanted to form a Non-Traditional Student Club and wanted to speak with me. I walked into the room and, sure enough, they qualified to be in a non-traditional organization, ranging in age from seventeen to sixty-seven. I asked the qualifications for membership, and they said they would perform due diligence and see if like organizations existed in colleges and universities across the country. I asked to be invited back once research was finished and they were ready to advertise the club within the college.

A month later the students were ready to report their findings. They indicated such organizations existed and membership eligibility was all over the map. I asked what the proposed requirements would bc for Red Rocks students. Their answer: "If students believe they are non-traditional, they are welcomed." They gave an insightful example that reflected the mission of community colleges: "If a student meets the profile that defines the traditional student: recent high school graduate, fulltime baccalaureate major, but he/she is the first in family to attend college, they probably consider themselves to be non-traditional." I agreed, gave my blessing, and thanked them for their initiative. One year later the unofficial leader of the group, a woman in her mid-forties who hadn't been in education since high school, discovered she was a math whiz and received a scholarship to our higher education colleague across town, the Colorado School of Mines, one of the most prestigious engineering schools in the world.

From the oldest students to the youngest, I was also supported by the *Bubble Bears*. RRCC has a wonderful design feature. There is a long and wide hallway that connects the largest facilities of the campus. The major administrative and student services are on both sides of the hallway, with a large floor-to-ceiling window that looks out on the foothills and provides a place to view the resident herd of deer that would come to visit.

The college has an award-winning childcare program, open to the public, and facilities that house an Early Childhood academic program. On any given day we would see a line of children, holding hands, walking to the other end of the building to get pieces of wood from the carpentry shop, or going to the bookstore, or hoping to see the herd of deer. They viewed the campus as an extension of their classrooms. Their trek never failed to brighten the faces of students and employees.

The President's Office was just off the hallway and located mid-building. One day, in my first month at the college, I returned to my office and saw twelve small children standing outside my office, turning the pages of a large dictionary that set on a small stand. I greeted them and asked if they would like to come into my office. Their teacher thought that was a great idea, but little did I know I was beginning the process of being adopted. They inventoried my office and immediately found the bowl of root beer candies I kept on my conference table. I always offered visitors a beer when they came in, and they were hoping they might be included. I told them their teacher would have to get their parents' permission. Soon, and a few stops later, we became fast friends. The early childhood model used in the program grouped students by age and treated them as a family. They would stay together the whole time they were in the program, until they left for kindergarten. It was explained they could choose the name of their family. They chose to be called the *Bubble Bears*, and I became an honorary member. I was invited to presentations and ceremonies, and frequently to lunch, always careful to choose a tie I wasn't too concerned about using again.

My parking spot was at the end of the building, just in front of the childcare playground. Every time I pulled into the campus I hoped it was play time for the children. As I walked toward the building entrance I would be spotted by a Bubble Bear who would scream: "Dr. Reno, Dr. Reno," and the class would charge the fence calling my name, asking me where I was going, what they had been doing that day, and when was I coming to lunch again? There was no better way to start my on-campus day.

One day I got a call from the Director of the program. She asked if I would come to the next Parent Advisory meeting. She had received calls wanting to know who this "Dr. Reno" was their child was talking about. We both laughed, I attended, told the parents how beautiful their children were, and how much my family membership meant to me, and how much I would miss them when they went off to kindergarten the following year. They thanked me for my involvement. I couldn't have asked for a better institution to begin my career as a college president.

* * *

Ending up in San Antonio was one of those: "If I had turned left instead of right at the end of the hallway

I would have missed out on one of the most satisfying professional periods of my career." Denver was hosting a national community college conference, and I went to the Convention Center to assist where I could, hoping to run into old friends and colleagues. It didn't take long. I walked down a hall, turned right, and ran into a former colleague from Florida, Dr. Terry Kelly. Dr. Kelly had been a long-time administrator at Miami-Dade Community College, and a near neighbor of Broward CC. He was the new Chancellor of the Alamo Community College District in San Antonio and was excited about the building projects they were about to begin, including a new college. My polite listening turned to active interest. "A brand-new college?" My interest must have been obvious, and Terry asked if I would be interested in applying. I knew Terry – everyone in the Florida community college system, and many from across the country knew Terry. He had a unique and magnetic personality and was a community college pioneer and a passionate advocate for the mission of quality access. I still had much to learn, and Dr. Kelly was someone to learn from.

I interviewed and got the position. I had intended to become the longest-serving President of Red Rocks Community College, but building a college was an exceedingly rare opportunity I could not let pass. A new college, a new part of the country, new communities, new friends and colleagues, a new culture, a new challenge. How many get the chance to incorporate all they have learned, spanning a whole career, into a new opportunity and the resources to make it happen?

My resume was strong in the areas of campus start-ups and facility and program development, but nothing close to providing leadership in the development and construction of a comprehensive community college. I am of that generation where institutions grew in stages, usually over decades: old K-12 facilities, storefronts, permanent sites, classroom and lab buildings – with arts and health/physical/athletic facilities to follow as resources became available.

A bond issue provided 250 acres and a $135 million budget. After a failed bond election, 125 community presentations, and a final bond passage, we were ready to design an interim facility; choose architectural firms and contractors; hire faculty, staff, and administrators; and develop the support and involvement of the ten communities the new college would be serving. We would also need to coordinate programmatic and construction activities with district personnel and the four existing colleges, and begin offering a full schedule of courses under the banner of an institution yet to be named. Who could ask for a more rewarding finale?

I brainstormed with the existing staff ways of formalizing community involvement and support. I was given names and historical events from the past ten years that had to be considered because of previous involvement before my arrival. I was warned that if we didn't involve or recognize all the prominent community members who had been advocating for the new college, there might be a problem. It soon became obvious feelings would be hurt, and we were not sure whose they might be, or how influential they might be in getting the college built. I decided to advertise a community breakfast, open to anyone who might want to be a part of the college's development or were just curious about the project.

We didn't know what to expect. Over one hundred people showed up. Thankfully, we had ordered breakfast tacos for 150. I developed a proposal to establish three community advisory committees: 1) Partnerships, 2) Programs, and 3) Design. We proposed each committee be co-chaired by a community member and a college liaison representative. Committee membership was open to any interested in participation. Seventy-five signed up wanting to get involved.

When people move into a new leadership position they usually inherit the people who work there, for good or bad. But the opportunity to hire all new employees is such a rarity that it needs to be shared. In addition to building an institution, we were building a culture. Our new VP for Academic Affairs, Dr. Beth Lewis, suggested our tagline: "Right from the Start." It adorned every document and was what everyone remembered and used as we debated and established operational guidelines and made decisions. Mission statements are notoriously hard to remember. The tagline was brief, memorable, and meaningful.

I had a warehouse of best practices I looked forward to implementing. The overall goal was to make sure the college was going to be "comprehensive." Some states believe community colleges should be funded only for classrooms, offices, and labs. Funding for student activities and facilities was reserved for four-year colleges and universities, or funded decades later. I admired Texas because decision-makers and communities seemed to love and support their colleges and universities, including community colleges.

We lived with architects and contractors for three years, each with a vision of how things were to be done. We evolved from distinctly different cultures to a hybrid team passionate about fulfilling the promises of this unique opportunity. We presented ideas and they made them better. They presented proposals and we shaped them to our needs. We often surprised each other with ideas that no one else had ever considered. By bringing users into the process, for example, we turned a classroom into a demonstration nutrition program kitchen, added a gymnasium, an art gallery, an outdoor amphitheater, a jewelry design studio, a second music rehearsal room, and a rock-climbing wall. By the end of the three-year project we all deserved diplomas that read: *Doctorate in Higher Education, Architecture, and Construction.*

I learned early that no detail is too small to be significant. While we waited for the campus to be built we redesigned a vacant Albertsons grocery store into an award-winning storefront facility. After our first semester we had a student gathering to assess how we were doing in all areas of their education. We asked all the right questions that would help us build a new culture for a new college. I expected to hear comments about the wonderful faculty, the up-to-date facilities and equipment, and the quality of support services. All were mentioned, but the one that got the most attention was a comment by an older and respected student: "You know what I appreciate? The restrooms are always clean." There was total agreement amongst the students and a lesson learned beyond any proclamation I could have produced. No detail is too small. Key architectural features of Northeast Lakeview College included:

- As many glass walls, windows, and scenic views in faculty offices and classrooms as possible.
- Small group study areas in every facility that welcome and encourage small group assignments and student interaction.
- No traditional tablet arm desks. Tables are set in a U-shaped arrangement, with tables inside the "U." All students face a minimum of 50% of their classmates, and the faculty walk into the middle of the students in aisles that separated the two sections. No place to hide. Students love the dynamics.
- Separate, yet connected buildings. The buildings flow into each other.
- Open parking, first-come, first-serve. Even for the President.
- OPPORTUNITY MALL: The Student Services building has two functional areas, the business (Registrar, Bursar, counseling, financial aid, testing) and Student Life section (bookstore, cafeteria, game rooms, etc.). Connecting the two ends of the long hallway are offices that house extracurricular opportunities: Honors, International Education, Veterans' Affairs, University Transfer Center, student employment,

Learning Communities, intramurals, and student organizations. Social engineering at its best. Students pass through the Opportunity Mall multiple times per week. No excuse not to be involved.

- Hundreds of trees throughout the campus. Carefully and strategically placed.
- Berry-less trees and bushes. NLC has large and attractive plazas and walkways, Berries attract birds and birds leave a mess.
- Bird-less buildings. I instructed faculty, staff and architects to visit entrances to local attractive and historic buildings. Though impressive, many are avoided because of the pigeon droppings. Impossible to keep clean. The design of every building brought to our meetings was closely reviewed for potential pigeon roosts. The possibilities were designed out.
- A singular architectural feature that represents the community. The singular architectural focal point of the community is the "Taj Mahal," located at the entrance to Randolph AFB, dubbed the "West Point of the Air" when it opened in the late 1920s. The NLC tribute tower is located at the main entrance to the college, as a feature of the library.
- $5,000 gum removal machine. As stated, NLC has beautiful plazas and walkways. Go to any building, historic or not, and you will see round and dark remnants of gum three feet from a trash can. I vowed that when I became King that

would become a felony. I Googled "gum removal machine" and found what I was looking for. At certain times of the year the machine comes out and the areas look brand new.

At every employee orientation I shared a truism I observed during my thirty-plus years in community colleges: "Institutions begin to lose their way when employees believe it exists to serve them." I follow that statement with: "We are all temporary stewards of our institution." I wasn't aware at the time that this statement struck such a positive chord that it was embossed on the NLC official Challenge Coin (Google "Challenge Coin" to understand its significance in a military community). I end with the observation that every day all employees have an opportunity to positively affect the lives of others, no matter their position at the institution.

I appropriated a Commencement tradition from Red Rocks Community College where graduates were given a 3 X 5 card where they would spell their names phonetically, list future plans, and thank someone for helping them to reach this point in their lives. The students hand the presenter their card, walk across the stage, and the audience hears "thank yous" to parents and relatives, spouses and children, friends, classmates, faculty, staff, security guards who welcomed them in the parking lot and directed them to the right building, custodians who acknowledge them every morning, and cafeteria workers who ask how their day had gone. I reminded new employees that for many students, because of previous personal and academic histories, the initial walk into the college is a frightening journey. My advice to returning students was to reinforce that "Living longer counts." Being at the college was their proof.

12. TRAGEDY and EDUCATION

They do not belong together.

I wish I were able to say my career was a forty-year honeymoon. It wasn't and there were times institutions, students, and employees were damaged by events never trained for or imagined. I was four months into my presidency at Red Rocks Community College, in Lakewood, Colorado, and a few miles from Columbine High School. Students and employees had personal connections with Columbine. Many attended, some had children enrolled, some had friends or family working at the school. The tragedy on April 20, 1999, was not news. It was our community, our families, our lives.

We set up televisions in all major open areas. As the horror unfolded we debated as to what to communicate to the evening college. Few employees went home. Many stayed to greet, advise, counsel. We posted communications on every classroom door and attempted to contact every evening faculty member. We offered options: cancel class, meet with students who wanted to talk about what happened, request professional counselors. We also asked faculty to announce that college-wide forums would take place the next day. In addition to our trained faculty and staff, professional grief counselors and facilitators would be in attendance.

The day event was standing room only. The agenda was structured, but the events of the previous day took over. Stories of being bullied led to other stories, questions about future security were a great concern, and overwhelming grief took place beyond the meeting and throughout the year. The need to be heard became the agenda. Faculty were encouraged to use class meetings as they saw fit – academics or continued discussions. We also scheduled an all-college employee meeting, addressing many of the same issues.

The specter of Columbine hung over the college for a very long time, and never went away. It was the beginning of an underlying sickness we are still waiting to be addressed. We established *Columbine Remembrance Scholarships* recognizing outstanding students whose qualities went beyond academics, and remembering those who were lost in the tragedy.

***

In mid-October 2008, Northeast Lakeview College (NLC) was scheduled to move its storefront library and become the first operational building on the permanent campus the following week. On the 13th an adjunct librarian walked into the storefront library, walked up to the circulation counter, was asked why he was coming in so early, took out large earmuffs and put them on, took out a pistol and shot the newest faculty librarian five times. He went to a table and laid down the gun and sat, waiting for police to arrive. Medical help arrived but nothing could be done. Devin Zimmerman was dead.

Crowds and media formed out front and were roped off from the entrance. Our Director of College Relations arrived to help with media relations. Our first step was to contact his wife, but we were unsuccessful. An hour later she came to the campus, and I had to tell her what happened. It was one of the most difficult moments I have ever faced. I had an hour to rehearse but don't know what came out of my mouth. I had no answers and could provide little comfort for the senseless act. She apologized for being late. She was coming from the doctor to surprise Devin with the announcement they were expecting their first child.

The shooter was in his early sixties and a long-standing member of his community, just having finished performing in a community theater production. His wife was the Dean of Learning Resources at one of the other colleges. Devin had been with us less than a year and had established a positive reputation with staff and faculty, and especially students, of being knowledgeable and helpful. He was a great fit for the new library, the new college, the developing culture. Most of the employees of the new college had been hired within a year of each other. They were a family, and a family member had been murdered, for reasons never shared or understood.

We cancelled classes for the next day, scheduling an all-college meeting to cry, comfort, share, explain, and remember. We scheduled an open meeting for students and community for the next day for the same purpose. We then voiced our tributes and goodbyes at the funeral service. A few days later we moved into the new library and formed a group to discuss how we wanted to remember Devin. The library staff asked if the Library Instruction classroom could be named after him because that was his favorite part of the job, ensuring that students were fully aware of what was available and how it could be accessed. As the campus was being built-out we also designed a seating area around a large live oak tree behind the library that would be called the Reading Tree, initiated by the tragedy and dedicated to all Northeast Lakeview employees who had passed away while still working at the college.

No one can be prepared for events as described. I offer no practical advice other than to be administratively, organizationally, and emotionally prepared for any emergency. That is the easy part. Every event will be unique, requiring the ability to present strength, compassion, and leadership throughout the crises. You will need to be accessible 24/7, looked to for empathy, sympathy, and difficult and quick decisions. You will need a soft heart and thick skin. You will be the face of the institution to the community and the media. Your leadership role will never be more visible or more important.

The tragic irony of educational institutions being the favored sites for mass murder is impossible to reconcile. The national commitment of a free education for all, a necessary requirement for any country aspiring to be "of the people, by the people, and for the people" is under siege by those who do not value their own lives or those of others. Some can be explained away by the mental conditions of the murderers, but many cannot. Those are the ones that force us to consider what familial and societal influences may have played a role. Finding out potential causes still is not enough to answer the unanswerable.

As I looked for answers, I remembered one of my favorite movies from a half century earlier, *Zorba the Greek* (1964), based on Nikos Kazantzakis' acclaimed 1946 novel about a slowly developing and transformative relationship between a poor, yet memorable character who believes life is lived by following one's instincts and emotions. His reluctant friend, Basil, is a British academic returning to his ancestral home on Crete who keeps his emotions deeply buried. At a pivotal event in the book both are devastated by the senseless murder of an attractive widow by the men of a village who resent her dismissal of their offers of marriage, but who had shown interest in Basil. At the height of their grief Zorba shouts at his friend, asking why the young must die, and what good are books at the time of inexplicable tragedy? Basil quietly responds: "They tell me about the agony of men who can't answer questions like yours." His response voices all I have not been able to articulate over the past twenty-three years

April 29, 2018: **COLLATERAL DAMAGE**

Now is the [summer] of our discontent when public servants again hope citizens will forget the latest mass tragedy so they can continue to please donors and obey ethically detached leaders. Columbine, Virginia Tech, Sandy Hook, Aurora, Orlando, Las Vegas, Stoneman Douglas High School, the Capital Gazette, Gilroy, El Paso, Dayton and other mass and singular tragedies, too painful and numerous, weave an ugly pattern of a troubled society into the once rich fabric of common ideals and purpose. We mourn victims and damn perpetrators, but do we consider the depth and breadth of the collateral damage that accompanies all tragedies?

- In an instant, families are torn apart, and their individual and collective futures are emotionally and psychologically shattered.
- Meaningful relationships, with profound future possibilities, evaporate.
- Permanent guilt is created – with family, friends, and survivors replaying the timing of fateful decisions.
- Anniversary and milestone dates that once signaled a celebration now resurrect pain and memories of lost potential. Children who once anticipated school as a rite-of-passage now harbor hidden fears in ways adults cannot comprehend, nor alleviate. Childhood innocence and joy are stolen.
- Our historical commitment to universal education has evolved to an environment and profession we never planned for or imagined.
- Our freedom and obligation to speak and publish harsh truths are threatened at the highest levels of government.
- Our once unshaken faith in our treasured Republic is diminished by the actions of those who govern, but who avoid responsibility to serve and protect.

The challenges in addressing solutions for our violent society are daunting, but we must first identify and elect people of good will and courage who are committed to finding common ground to support the common good. If solutions must have an "either/or" outcome, we get nowhere. Collateral damage is a multiplier of tragedy. It isn't temporary or generational, it is eternal – the damage that keeps on taking.

Eric Reno
Fort Collins, CO

13. The TAUGHT and the LEARNED

The evolution of a "Street Scholar"

I wanted to know what everyone else knew and what most would never know. I am not a scholar, but realized how formal and informal education contributed to the professional I became. I have never understood those who give their "self" up and let life happen to them, and those who give their "self" over to charismatic leaders and vague causes, losing their identity and independence in the process. I understand and accept passive ignorance, which can be cured by education. But active and purposeful ignorance requires a conscious decision to avoid or dismiss the benefits of education and personal responsibility.

Two of the major elements of education are what is taught and what is brought. If my education had been confined to wisdom distributed in school, I would still be busting concrete blocks. I failed miserably in the classroom but grew by following my natural curiosity and budding interests that were preparing me for the grail: adulthood and a life of meaningful experiences. The paths of the taught and the learned never seemed to cross. One was necessary, the other seductive, promising the possible over the practical. But I also realized, much later, that my high school teachers did their best to teach me, but I didn't bring much to the educational desk. I was fighting the battle of the hormones, and the hormones were winning. The only positive reinforcement I received prior to high school graduation was at my senior year exit interview when I was told I had potential. "Next student please."

I was hopeless in math, though very good with numbers. Everything had to be practical; the theoretical was a mystery. I could calculate baseball batting averages, a pitcher's earned run average (ERA), and a hitter's slugging percentage in my head, but I barely completed the math requirement for a high school diploma. Our final math teacher was John Yost, who I saw as a teacher and a mathematician and someone to be made fun of because of the ever-present yellow chalk dust surrounding his right front pants' pocket.

His claim to fame, from our perspective, came from our English class assignment to memorize the first eighteen-line General Prologue to Chaucer's *Canterbury Tales* – in Middle English! We didn't understand the poetry in Modern English. Our English teacher said that once memorized it would never be forgotten. As we entered our math classroom we loudly shared our laughter and frustration at the idea we would forever remember the assignment. Mr. Yost asked us to take out our homework and open our math book and proceeded to recite Chaucer's General Prologue, in Middle English, all eighteen lines:

"Whan that Aprille with his shoures soote,
The droghte of March hath perced to the roote,

And bathed every veyne in swich licóur
Of which vertú engendred is the flour . . . . "

Deadly quiet and dropped jaws followed. Then we began our math. Sixty years later I have no problem remembering the recitation – in Middle English.

Prior to the final exam he scheduled a volunteer study session for any who wanted assistance. I needed to attend and was surprised when he ended the math and asked what our plans were following graduation. He became a person, and I responded immediately to this gentle and concerned man. I grew up a little during that hour. Four years later, following my discharge from the Air Force, I walked into my College Review Math course at the community college and was introduced to our teacher, Mr. John Yost. I was sure he wouldn't remember me. I was not a memorable student. As the class was dismissed he called my name and asked me to stay, wanting to know what I had been doing, what brought me back to school, and what were my future plans. He was a person this time around, and I did my best to be a math student, though I was still looking for the value of "X."

As I worked diligently to achieve my goal of becoming the first college graduate in our family, I realized choices had to be made and a direction was required. There was more than just getting the "collegiate experience." I was in my sophomore year and needed to declare a major. I had no obvious professional passions, nor aptitudes, so I decided on English. After all, I had lived in England and loved to read. The idea of being an English major having anything to do with my professional future never crossed my mind. A career in education? It didn't occur to me for another seven years.

The person who had the biggest influence in my decision to major in English was Harry Crews (1935-2012). I got him early before he became a national literary figure. I was in my last semester at the junior college where he held forth every semester in his *Introduction to Creative Writing*. I had attempted to register for two previous semesters, but his classes filled immediately. I finally got in. He was not the cult-like figure people knew much later at the University of Florida, and in the monthly pages of *Esquire* and *Playboy*. He was clean cut, wore a coat and tie, was Paul Newman good-looking, and spellbinding in the classroom. He told stories about his life, the lives of other writers, and the craft of writing. Writing was his life, and it became clear that if he couldn't write he would die. He shared works in progress. He was probably the first practicing writer any of us had ever met. I hung on every sentence, learning what I couldn't put into words. The highlight of the semester was when he shared a letter of acceptance for his first novel, *The Gospel Singer*, for publication. One of my most prized possessions is a copy that he signed: "To Rick Reno: Take care of your talent; you are one of the real ones. Harry Crews."

I loved my four years of academic sampling, discovering what I didn't know, what I didn't want to know, and how much I knew I didn't know I knew. I also discovered I had an academic "death wish" that was about more than academics. I had a life-long fear of public speaking. The audience went out of focus and my words mumbled during verbal assignments. When I began my administrative career there were opportunities I avoided because of the additional public forums I would encounter. Which begs the question: why did I enroll in a course titled, *Reader's Theater*, during my junior year at Florida Atlantic University?

The class was composed of theater majors who knew each other by name and reputation. The course was taught by the Head of the department. I was conspicuous by my presence. Everyone else seem to know the drill: select a work, introduce the segment you are going to present, and apply your theatrical skills to your reading. I left the first meeting terror stricken. The second unanswered question remains: why did I stay? Maybe it was because I lived at the London theater every weekend for those years of my Air Force posting and believed that appreciation would translate into performance. My classmates were friendly and considerate, and even observed I was creative in selecting works no one else ever considered. But I survived, improved, made friends, and even carried a spear in a production that semester.

My final suicidal academic experience took place in the semester prior to graduation. I had finally worked up the courage to enroll in a philosophy course taught by a campus legend, Dr. Robert Schwarz. He was also known as someone who did not suffer fools lightly. He had escaped Vienna in 1939 through the *Kindertransport* program that saved the lives of many Jewish children from Nazi persecution. Students knew they were in the presence of a scholar. No "easy A" to be had. Every week Dr. Schwarz would offer students opportunities for extra credit by placing philosophical questions on the board and asking students to volunteer to address and present their findings to the class the following week.

We had the whole week to research the complexity of the topics before volunteering. I religiously avoided the opportunities. Topics were snapped up by the end of every week, except for one that students avoided all semester, even the philosophy majors. Dr. Schwarz announced near the end of the semester there was one opportunity remaining to volunteer for the "avoided one." He asked if there were any takers. Students looked around the room wondering who might have found the courage. As I looked around I felt my right arm rising, and looked to confirm that it was mine. Expressions of surprise populated the room. Dr. Schwarz looked at me and said: "Mr. Reno. I look forward to your presentation."

The issue again is not that I volunteered, but why? *Reader's Theater* all over again. I had forced myself to achieve beyond my comfort level. How else would I grow? I spent more time preparing for that fifteen-minute presentation than I had the rest of the course. I was dazed and confused but initial comprehension slowly surfaced. As I walked to the front of the class I saw all seats were filled. I presented my findings, turning to Dr. Schwarz every time I made a point, silently asking if I was close to being perceptive, or should I take a seat before I embarrassed myself any further? Fortunately, he nodded with every turn, and I finished my presentation.

These were minor examples of unexplained and uninformed behaviors. Fortunately, they involved only me. More serious choices were made that involved the lives of others, including loved ones, and the future of institutions. There are consequences for decisions. I am not sure whether I should be praised or questioned. Only the results count.

***

I will always consider myself to be a teacher, no matter the position or responsibilities. In positions of authority, our presence, our actions, and our communications are silently observed and evaluated. We are a package of what we say and what we do. They had better match. I grew into my teaching effectiveness due mainly to the fact I was once one of those students silently daring teachers to make me interested in what they had to say.

After a digestive time-period, "literature" became life guides, wise and practical. I was able to extract the essence from books, stories, movies, epochs of history. I was touched by James Agee's novel, *A Death in the Family*, a story told through the eyes of a young and only child. That novel was even more poignant at thirty-five following the death of our first born and the time to reflect on the death of my father. I was a different reader. It was a different story.

My freshman and sophomore students represented a variety of majors fulfilling the Humanities general education requirement. My job was to provide insights, application, and appreciation. When I taught I wanted to give students permission to leave the mundane and welcome the humanity.

In one of the last courses I was able to teach, our text was the *Norton Anthology of American Literature.* I discovered that someone I had hired to teach part-time years before had two poems in the anthology. I was in my first year as a department head and Judith Ortiz Cofer (1952-2016) stopped by my office with her newly minted M.A. in English from my alma mater, Florida Atlantic University. She had all the qualities a department head was looking for in a new hire: she was charismatic, articulate, and passionate about her teaching area. Alas, she wasn't with us for long. One day she asked if I would read her poetry. Her talent was destined for other places. She taught for a few semesters and moved on, but we stayed in touch until she went to the University of Georgia and became a distinguished professor and a national figure, publishing poetry and fiction along the way.

As I prepared learning activities for the poetry segment I wondered if Judy (I was one of the few people allowed to call her "Judy" instead of "Judith") would be willing to do a phone segment for my night class and talk all things poetry. I got through immediately, we caught up, and she agreed to committing an hour for the class. Fortunately, though fearing poetry, the students loved Judy's two poems. I instructed them to each prepare a question for her when we connected the following week. There was no format for the phone discussion. Judy took each question, elaborated, made it personal, and made it relevant to their lives. We went beyond the one hour and when the phone was cradled we debriefed. They were in love with Judy and poetry and transformed by how she converted academic dread into something they saw as necessary for a full life. They couldn't wait to get home and start writing.

When I began my career I felt obligated to make sure my students were armed with the requisite literary terminology to survive if they were kidnapped by a rogue book club. I structured a portion of my final exams into two sections: 1) a list of literary terms (simile, metaphor, alliteration, personification, allegory, point-of-view, etc.), and 2) samples of each taken from pieces of literature. Students had to define the terms and match them with the bits of literature. After all, this was the type of exam and academic accountability I had been subject to, but also a sure literature appreciation killer. That semester I changed how I taught non-major survey courses. I passed out the exam, listened to the groans, and gave them ten minutes to read it over.

I then asked them to stop what they were doing and announced I had divided the class into equal sized groupings. I asked them to arrange their group into a circle and take that portion of the exam as a single entity, submitting one exam whose answers and grade were applicable to all members. I saw unexpected learning taking place. Groups structured their process in different ways, but discussions were active, instructive, and passionate. Mimi-lectures, civil differences, and final decisions were reached and submitted. I left time in the class so we could go over the exams. As correct answers were announced, questions and alternative possibilities were debated. Finally, I announced everyone was receiving an "A" for that 50% of the final, learning what I had hoped for, and what they had dreaded.

October 2015
San Francisco State University
English Department

Colleagues:

I'm not sure this is the best way to share my long overdue appreciation for my two years (1970-71) at San Francisco State University, but here goes. As a newly minted English major from Florida Atlantic U. I came to SF to make my corporate mark and was enrolled in a management training program for a major airline. After three years I realized I was not corporate material but not sure what I could do with my educational background. I had gotten into the habit of sharing my passion for literature with co-workers and wondered if I had the "right stuff" to get a masters from the university across the street. I submitted my minimum-level GRE scores and was accepted provisionally. I felt surrounded by future Pulitzer winners who could find insights and significance in every word and line of every reading assignment. I sat silent, hoping one day to rise to their level of academic comprehension.

Though at times overmatched I was mesmerized by the quality and passion of the teachers who challenged and inspired me to stay with the program, beginning with my first class (Dickens) when Dr. Middlebrook swept into our night class in his well-traveled full-length leather coat, sparse beard/moustache, and naturally curly locks – appearing to be either Fagin or Bill Sykes. To that point I had never enjoyed nor appreciated Dickens, but that was changed forever. I was terrified of Dr. Stanley Tick, but he dared me to rise to his expectations and rewarded my hard work with praise and constructive criticism. Robin Gajdusek peeled away the subtle layers of my literary and adolescence mentor, Ernest Hemingway, and made the literary swamp of Faulkner's South understandable. And Dr. Robinson taught us the skills we would need to teach undergrads how to write.

I managed to complete the program and passed my oral exam because of my "potential." I never caught up with my brilliant peers but discovered I needed time for all I had absorbed to fall into place. I knew I would never be doctoral material but discovered I had the ability to make every piece of literature discussed in my lower division survey courses relevant and applicable to the lives of students. That became the key to my teaching success and my students' new-found appreciation of a subject many dreaded.

I share my compressed experience hoping to reinforce what you already know: we can go broke predicting the futures of students who come through our institutions. I share mine for what it may be worth. My eternal gratitude.

Dr. Eric Reno, President
Northeast Lakeview College
Class of 1971

Early in my teaching career I invited a friend to sit in on one of my classes. It was an evening *Film as Literature* course, and the after-viewing discussion was immediate and dynamic. Afterwards we went for a drink, and I asked if he enjoyed the class. He was impressed, but asked a question I had never considered: "Do you know the answers to the questions you ask the students?" I wasn't sure. Later analysis confirmed I did, but I also discovered my responses were more creative and thorough if I was caught by surprise. I was not a lecturer, but rather a responder. I became aware of the importance of a balance between what students wanted to know and what I wanted them to learn.

I also learned to feature the gifts of my students in showcasing expectations and possibilities. Presenting the words of professionals as models can be illuminating but also intimidating. I kept a file of student work (with their permission) to share prior to an assignment and reinforced the fact this was the work of a peer. The first writing assignment in Freshman Comp I was to write a "personal experience paper," hoping this would be the least intimidating. The instructions were to write about something meaningful from their lives. It didn't have to be significant to the reader, but the reader must see why it was significant to the author.

Then the magic of teaching and learning begins, especially when the wide range of ages, experience, and maturity are under the same tent. Freshman Composition is usually feared – the great unknown. I make it clear to students their final grade will reflect the level of writing skills at the end of the semester. They will not be penalized at the beginning for what they did not know. Beyond what skills they are taught, they are encouraged to see classmates as mentors and editors and to assume those roles in exchange. Chances are taken, fear is lifted, and basic and advanced skills are developed. At a minimum they will know what is necessary for academic success. Their responsibility is to practice and apply what they have been taught.

June 3, 2011: ACCOUNTABILITY IS FINE, BUT IT WON'T REPLACE GREAT TEACHERS

Lately I've been suffering from an advanced case of "retireitis." Symptoms include envisioning your own retirement party while attending another's, deciding which suits and ties you will keep and which you will donate to the theater department, being a little more forthcoming in saying what you really think – and wondering what will be the latest "proof of institutional/academic effectiveness indicator" required by the State before retirement.

I truly understand the need for documenting institutional effectiveness and academic outcomes, the need to identify and replicate best practices, and the need to establish a "culture of evidence." But while every segment of higher education struggles to identify its most meaningful accountability measures, the challenge is greatest at community colleges.

For many community college students a commitment to higher education requires a complex balancing of schoolwork, jobs, and families, and comes with a wide range of personal, professional, economic, educational, and cultural demographic histories. And unfortunately, labels stubbornly stick. Once students have been labeled as failures because they failed to complete educational goals within a certain time-period, or they dropped out for any reason – they are doomed to remain in "failure purgatory." Most community-college accountability standards begin with the academic records of only first-time students. Community colleges enroll a significant percentage of people who were once cited as academic failures, but have returned to continue and complete their education.

My institution recently honored a student who enrolled in a community college upon graduation from high school but dropped out for health reasons. She was immediately laid to rest as a "failure." She returned fifteen years later as a wife and mother of five, became an officer in the Phi Theta Kappa honor society, a founding member of the Education Club, and went on to receive a full scholarship to an outstanding faith-based university. Her failure, though, remains in the accountability database. How do we get credit for this born-again success, emblematic of the mission and value of a community college system in the first place? I have tired of attempting to get an accountability system that acknowledges the possibility of educational resurrection.

What concerns and disappoints me most is the lack of recognition and emphasis on those elements of education that are impossible, or difficult at best, to measure. Over the years we've been cautioned that we are moving from the "sage on the stage" to the "guide on the side." I'm not sure these roles are incompatible but wonder if those who dismiss the "sage on the stage" ever had a great teacher. Most students I have encountered over the past 35 years attribute their positive educational experiences to the quality of their teachers.

Another symptom of "retireitis" is going through old files. I recently came across an op-ed piece I wrote for our local newspaper in 1997. Its relevance to this discussion struck me as not having changed much, and as being even more relevant today. Here is an abbreviated version.

After five years of trying to arrange my schedule so I could get back into the classroom I finally volunteered to teach an *Introduction to Literature* course that met at night. My students' motives for enrolling ranged from needing the requirement to "I love literature" to "My wife says I read too much technical material and need to broaden my horizons." Midway through the semester a student came in, obviously excited about something, and shared with the class that he had attended a frequent get-together of his wife's friends and there was a discussion that referenced an author or literary work from our class. He said that for the first time he was able to participate and contribute. That was all they discussed on the drive home.

The fifteen weeks that followed were filled with hard work, false starts, steady growth, shared discovery, and moments of magic. I was reminded that an education, in addition to the acquisition of skills and knowledge, includes the appreciation of newly learned subject matter, changes of attitudes, and sudden and unexpected insights. The grades I assigned at the end of the semester did not necessarily reflect what I believed the students took away from the course. From the perspective of evolving from a group of total strangers to a community of learners, they each deserved an "A," but I know that it doesn't work that way. It's important to document what students know, but I wish it always meant that we've graded them on how much they have learned.

Now, almost 15 years later, I will start planning for retirement, which I hope will include teaching. That way I may continue to experience the true and hard-to-quantify magic of the educational experience – dependent, of course, on my ability to keep my productive grade rate at an acceptable level, and steadily increasing student retention, persistence, and completion rates.

Published in *The Chronicle of Higher Education*
Eric Reno, Founding President, Northeast Lakeview College
San Antonio, TX

***

My final teaching opportunity occurred while shoveling snow. When I retired in 2014 I was recovering from serious medical issues, including open heart surgery in June. In December we had a heavy snowstorm, and at the age of seventy-two, and against all common sense, I grabbed a shovel and headed out to clear the driveway. We had new neighbors across the cul-de-sac. Though I had waved at folks entering and leaving, we had not been formally introduced. A few minutes after I had begun shoveling, a delightful young lady came bounding across the deep snow, shovel in hand. We made short work of the snow, and I invited her in for coffee and the opportunity to meet family. I asked her to invite her family over, mother and brother. Dr. Christina Minihan and I, and our families, became personal friends and professional colleagues.

Dr. Minihan is a Professor of Tourism and Journalism at Colorado State University and was named a *Best Teacher of the Year for 2022* recipient by the Colorado State University Alumni Association. This was no surprise to me. I had been in her classes and knew how her students felt about her.

We have talks about the joys and challenges of teaching in higher education. She schedules community members to guest in her courses, and I was honored to be included. It is a day on my calendar I look forward to every semester. Not sure what might be of interest or value to university students, I decided to tell my story. My jagged pathway seemed to resonate and rewarding discussions followed. After a few semesters Dr. Minihan asked if I would put some of my talking points in writing, to be distributed to students prior to my visit. They will be poised to comment, ask, and share.

A question on Dr. Minihan's final exam asks students to choose insights gleaned from community presenters. My presentation and observations are frequently mentioned. I was someone who knew what they were going through – their fears, confusion, indecision. I was someone of note who had succeeded, despite the uncertainties they currently faced.

March 17, 2020

Dear Dr. Minihan:
Professor of Tourism and Journalism
Colorado State University

Per your request I am providing lessons learned by having lived seventy-seven years that hopefully complement my presentation on March 9th. But first, I would like to thank you for the opportunity to meet with your students, and to compliment your class for their attentiveness and willingness to actively and thoughtfully contribute to the discussion. For what it may be worth is a partial listing, in no particular order, of what I have observed and hopefully put into practice.

LESSONS LEARNED

- The measure of a life should reflect who you are, not necessarily what you do.
- Every stop in life creates a new start.
- We all are walking resumes and works in progress.
- The person we were growing up is not necessarily the person we will become.
- The greater exposure to the wonders of the world and the talents and character of those you encounter will have a dramatic impact on maturity.
- Enjoy and explore the talents and genius of those who:
  - think beyond our ability to analyze and digest a truly complex world.
  - create, produce, and perform that which educates, fulfills, provides joy, and reminds us of the wonders and blessings of our humanity.
- Be curious, watch, listen, and read critically.
- The more you grow outside of your own senses enhances who you will become.
- Choose your friends wisely. People who do not reflect your or accepted behaviors love company. You may attempt to help them as they mature, but if they persist in destructive thoughts and behaviors, cut them loose.
- Discover your passion. The one life you have should not be wasted.
- Listen more than you talk.
- Believe in something of value.

- Everything you do in life is a learning experience. What you do with what you've learned is what is important.
- Develop behaviors that reflect who you are. Family, friends, and colleagues appreciate principled consistency in the person they love and admire.
- Never underestimate your ability to positively impact the lives of others by actions you take and behaviors you exhibit.
- Ideas are improved when they are shared with those you trust and respect.
- Don't let others tell you who you are. That is your responsibility.
- Celebrate joy and appreciate and practice appropriate humor.
- Life is a marathon, not a sprint. Prepare accordingly.
- Attractiveness is given. Beauty is earned.
- It is the journey, not always the destination.
- Everyone has opinions. Listen only to those who can back them up.
- Words can damage and destroy, or they can inspire and enlighten. Use them wisely.

After having shared my personal and professional career I end with a warning, and ask they pay close attention because they might one day face the same dilemma. I ask if they have been fearful about their futures, confused about their ability to compete in the world, fearful about making the right decisions, insecure about not having the social skills they envy in others, and wondering if they will be able to provide a happy and satisfying life for their future families? "Does that describe anybody?" Hands go up and heads nod. "Listen carefully to what I am about to say. If any of those issues describe you, past or present, I want you to be extremely careful. You too could end up as a college president."

***

INTERNATIONAL EDUCATION

Life-changing experiences usually cannot be predicted, but a few are sure things. The effect of international education on students, faculty, and staff are life-changing for many. I was born in the United States, but my adult life began in a foreign country. I learned more about my homeland by being away than I had while living in it. The Air Force based me in England for three years, taking a poor high school student and eventually turning me into an English major. The meaningful journey began there.

We encountered physical borders, exchanged and attempted to understand differing currencies, rearranged our phrase books, attempted different languages, and faced storied and confusing histories and cultures. In turn, I saw my country filtered through the eyes of others whose background spanned centuries, endless conflicts, physical and spiritual disasters, societal quakes and shifts, and artistic and scientific movements and discoveries that laid the foundation for the progress that followed.

My first experience in a non-English speaking country was in Germany where I had won tickets to fly to Frankfurt to see the Armed Forces European football championship game, involving our own Chicksands

Fighting Chicks. We flew in a WWII C-47 to Frankfurt. The C-47 was a DC-3 in civilian aviation and the backbone of modern commercial and military aviation with its introduction in the mid-1930s as the first twin-engine aircraft able to maintain flight on one engine.

We stowed our luggage and headed to the heart of the city and to the most recommended *biergarten*. When our waitress asked for our order we looked at each other and someone finally spoke up and said we wanted beer. I was new to beer drinking and said I would have what everyone else was having. I said: "How about a pitcher?" We all agreed. The waitress asked if we were sure that's what we wanted? Moments later she came back with four large pitchers of beer, what we assumed was one for our table and three for other tables. A pitcher was placed in front of each of us. Much later we calculated each pitcher held approximately two liters of beer. No one was brave enough to admit this was their first encounter with a liter of anything, and no one had the courage to say we had made a mistake. The evening was filled with *gemutlichkeit*. We made friends we couldn't understand, ate multiple varieties of *wursts*, and drank beer in volumes never before attempted. We managed to get back to the barracks, crashed onto our bunks, and asked on our way home who won the game.

International education became a major interest and activity during my forty-year professional career. Dr. Bill Greene taught history at Broward Community College and began summer trips abroad in the late 1960s that, over the years, grew into one of the largest and most respected international education programs in the nation. Dr. Greene became a full-time director and established programs and opportunities around the globe. My military time in England led to coordinating the College's Semester-in-London and Summer-in-Cambridge programs. Dr. Greene asked me to be involved in the establishment of programs in Malaysia and Singapore, where International Schools (operating on the British educational model) became affiliates of the American College and offered an American-style curriculum for non-citizens who were restricted from participating in the higher education systems of the host country.

I thought I knew much of the history of the Far East but had none of the experience. On my first Far East venture preconceptions were shattered. I was a born-again traveler. I was fascinated by the sights, sounds, history, cultures. So much to learn and so little time. My Western-centric body of knowledge faded and was absorbed into a larger world view. We stopped in Hong Kong for two days prior to business in Kuala Lumpur, Malaysia. I caught the shopping fever experienced by all new and gullible tourists and discovered that no matter the bargain I made on my purchases, I would find them at half that price at the next store. But I was always reminded by Dr. Greene that cost didn't matter: "Remember. You can never put a price on you wife's happiness." Dr. Greene was our leader. He got us on and off planes and through customs, to our hotels, and knew the location of every McDonald's in every city we visited.

Our first assignment in Malaysia was to visit the international school we had hoped to work with and meet with decision-makers. The Chinese Headmistress oriented us and indicated the final decision on a relationship would depend on a meeting with C.B., who owned the school and the hotel where we were staying. Dr. Greene suggested she call C.B. and set up a meeting as soon as possible. Her demeanor changed immediately; "You never contact C.B. He will contact us." We returned to the hotel and were informed to be at the front of the hotel at 7:30pm sharp, and we would be driven to dinner with C.B. At exactly 7:30pm three large Mercedes pulled up. Out jumped six Chinese linebackers who directed us to cars and seating. One of our party was guided to the front seat in the car ahead, and I saw him stumble when he got in. The doors slammed shut, locks automatically engaged, and we drove through the streets of Kuala Lumpur at highway speeds, with no more than a few feet between vehicles.

During the white-knuckle ride we discovered there were no handles on the inside of the doors, the window glass was an inch thick, and there were bulges in the suitcoats of our escorts. We entered an alley, went up three flights of stairs, and navigated hallways, with a linebacker at each juncture. We entered a banquet room that contained a large round table. We proceeded with formal introductions, the expensive cognac flowed, and the delicious food never ceased. We had received a briefing on etiquette within the Malaysian and Chinese cultures, and sure enough, the head of the fish was put before the senior member of our delegation. Though not a lover of seafood, he knew his responsibility, praising the delicacy all the way down. We also exchanged gifts, aware that any gift we presented should not exceed the value of the gift presented by the host.

It was a glorious evening, with all of us exceeding our food and drink capacity with ease. Business was never discussed. We didn't find out until the next day the agreement was a go. During the debrief I mentioned our ride to dinner and discovered our colleague in the front Mercedes had stumbled over a submachine gun sticking out from under the front seat, and the purpose of high speeds and close fenders was to ensure no one could come between the cars and isolate C.B. There was always a danger of the kidnapping of wealthy and powerful citizens. Our partnership began the following year.

I accompanied the first Broward Community College Semester-in-London students to their new institution in January 1977, the Ealing College of Higher Education. I was there to participate in the orientation process, meet with my British counterparts, and ensure the eight students were settled in with their host families. The January English weather was quite the contrast for eight young people from South Florida. Their enthusiasm went from the radiant to the gray and cold of the weather. I met with them the day before my departure and am convinced by their looks that if offered the opportunity, I would have had to find eight return tickets. But they stuck it out, I kept in touch with parents, and as we got closer to the end of the semester, feared we wouldn't be able to get them back. They were having too much fun, had made friends, had traveled extensively, and didn't want it to end.

They did return and Pat and I hosted a reunion party a month later. We heard humorous and inspirational stories and saw cherished pictures. They finally were around people who shared and appreciated what they had experienced. We kept in touch over the next few years, and I was able to confirm that seven of the eight majored and graduated in a subject directly influenced by their semester in London. The eighth student ended up marrying a young Englishman she had met during the semester, and moved to the UK. I believe that would count as a related outcome.

That first trip was satisfying in many ways. I took advantage of free time to visit old haunts. I exited the Tube near the Savoy Hotel, wanting to explore what I overlooked thirteen years before. I was approached by a young lady who asked directions to the Savoy. I told her three blocks further. "Oh my God. I've asked directions from a Yank!" She laughed and headed toward the hotel, occasionally looking back with a wave and a smile. I gave her my best British grin and returned her wave with my best royal effort. After years of trying I had finally passed as a native.

I also had the good fortune to help coordinate the State of Florida's *Summer in Cambridge* study-tour, held during the Cambridge Festival, usually in the month of July. University and community college students took courses taught by Cambridge faculty, plus the addition of programed tours on weekends. One weekend included matinee and evening productions of *A Midsummer Night's Dream* and *Macbeth* by the Royal Shakespeare Company at Stratford-Upon-Avon. Most students were familiar with Shakespeare only through having read a play in high school or studied one in a survey of British Literature course at college. Many asked if they needed to attend. I convinced them this was a "don't miss" opportunity they would regret not taking advantage of. I was seated behind the students at the matinee and was rewarded by their continuous laughter. Many said *Midsummer* was one of the funniest things they had ever seen, and couldn't wait to see a Tragedy. William would have been gratified.

Dr. Greene also ensured that college faculty and staff were given opportunities for international involvement. Their expertise was critical to the success of the many international partnerships, and provided many college employees with their first international travel. I was asked to return to Singapore to work with the English trained faculty on understanding American Higher Education, and the community college's systems and culture. They also requested a science faculty member to work with them on the design of curricula and the structure of accompanying lab requirements. Terry Hamilton was chosen. Terry was an admired senior faculty member who had never been west of the Mississippi River. He was approaching retirement age, with the experience and personality required for the assignment.

Terry was perfect for our objective, jumping right in, connecting with his international colleagues, and fully aware of this once-in-a-lifetime professional development opportunity. We were in Singapore during the 100th anniversary of the internationally famous Raffles Hotel (est. 1887). We decided to splurge, far beyond our *per diem*, and have dinner at Raffles. The setting was out of a British colonial movie, as we dined at the outdoor setting, the Raffles Courtyard, listened to stories of our Chinese waiter who was celebrating his 40th anniversary at Raffles, and enjoyed the most expensive and memorable dinner of our lives. We have commemorative anniversary menus, signed by our beaming waiter. Terry was hooked; he was a born-again educator. He was always ready to volunteer for another international adventure, and always ready to host international visitors at his home for the length of their stay at the college.

Through Dr. Greene I got involved with CCIS (College Consortium for International Studies) and was Board Chair for five years prior to retirement. CCIS was a consortium of over one hundred two-and four-year American institutions that offered semester-long programs, in cooperation with an international partner, on almost every continent. Those involved in international education are passionate about their responsibilities. The complexities and potential problems require an encyclopedic knowledge of national/international rules and regulations, and the diplomatic skills to navigate the concerns of apprehensive parents and college governing boards.

We were reminded every year of our mission at our annual conferences in Washington, D. C., and every third year at one of our international host institutions, when panels of students shared stories of their semester-long experiences. Though different in detail, the essence was the life-changing impact of their varied times. Their acclimation to their new international home always seemed less daunting than their re-adjustments upon their return home. They told wonderful anecdotes, laughed, shook their heads knowingly as fellow students shared their stories. They all felt homesick for their international home and felt isolated because there was no one who truly understood the special nature of the experience. One young lady from Vermont, who had spent a semester in Seville, Spain, shared her frustration that her childhood friends called it an evening and were home in bed, just about the time they would be deciding where to have dinner in Seville.

From my experience in England and my involvement in international education, we assumed our son, Patrick, would be interested in a study abroad opportunity. He didn't need convincing. He was ready to see the world beyond Colorado and chose Ireland. When we drove to the airport we discussed all the things he might want to do, and cautions I shared with all participating students. His mother chose not to see him off at the airport; the parting would have been more than she could have faced. The closer we got to departure the more concerned I became. He was still our eldest and only son, and the words I used to ease the concerns of parents whose children were going abroad seemed hollow. As he waved from the down escalator I became one of those parents, fearful and aware of all that could go wrong.

We waited for two days to hear from him. I knew how busy they would be, meeting host families and classmates from around the United States. We vowed to call if we had not heard from him by the third night. At 3:00am on the third night the phone rang. That terrible call all parents dread. The phone was on Pat's side of the bed, and she grabbed it and sat on the edge. "Hi Patrick," she said loudly, accompanied by a sigh of relief. But I sensed there was a problem. I indicated I wanted the phone. I was the expert. I knew who to call and what to do. The more I was shushed the madder I got. Was he in trouble, was he sick, didn't he get along with his host family? That could be changed. Then the final frustration. She shushed me one more time and turned to give Patrick the advice I believed should have come from me. "Patrick. Here is what you need to do. You put the white clothes in one pile and the colored ones in another."

His semester in Ireland was the life-changing experience we had hoped for. He became close to his host family and was idolized by their six-year-old son. He organized a trip to the Continent at Spring Break. He made friends with the Irish students by asking if he could scrimmage with the basketball team. They were honored that he was interested. Most of his American colleagues were from the northeast. I commented that, in addition to getting to know a foreign culture, he was also exposed to a part of America he had never visited.

I asked if he could tell any differences. He said they talked fast and were arrogant, but he got along and was making new friends.

We flew to Ireland at the end of his semester and met his host family and went out to dinner. Our first stop in Dublin was at the Guinness brewery. Patrick could pull a pint with the best. When it came time for goodbyes, Patrick's host family asked if they could have time alone with Patrick. The tears were evident. It is difficult and rewarding being a parent. He remains in contact with his host family these many years later.

From Ireland we returned to England to spend time in London. I drove the family to Chicksands to show off Dad's early years. After having to ask directions to someplace where I had spent three years of my life, we arrived at the front gate, parked, and approached a heavily guarded building. The base had reverted to the British in the 1990s but still had an intelligence mission. Veteran, spouse, and three children entered the building, and I introduced myself as having been based at Chicksands forty years before, and would there be any chance of driving around to show my family where I had lived, worked, and grown up? They apologized and stated that because of its classified functions, that would not be possible.

I put on my most forlorn face and headed for the door, stopped, turned, and asked: "It's been a long time. Which hill housed the elephant cage (the FLRN-9 antenna)? I was here when it was constructed." It had been gone for many years. The guards stopped what they were doing, reacting as though their office had just been invaded by a dinosaur, huddled for a few moments, and then said I could drive through but were not allowed to get out of the car. I gave a nostalgic tour for my family, pointing out the Priory, my dorm, where the baseball field had been, while being shadowed by an unmarked automobile, the intelligence function still at work.

My final professional involvement in international education, and my proximity to now-ancient history, took place in Budapest, Hungary in 1999. I was the only community college representative to attend the AUDEM (Alliance of [American] Universities for Democracy) annual conference. The focus of the presentations was to assess the progress of higher education in advancing democracy in the newly liberated countries. One of the prominent hosts was a professor at the university and member of the Hungarian Parliament, who took us on a tour of the Parliament building, one of the most impressive buildings I had ever seen. His history included participating in and escaping to the United States during the 1956 Hungarian uprising. He earned a doctorate from Columbia University and had a career in teaching, returning to Hungary in the 1980s to run for Parliament, and being elected. As we walked down the magnificent hallway I asked when he had first visited this historic governmental home. He stated: "In 1945 when I was interrogated in the basement by the Gestapo." I wish I had taken the opportunity to hear the rest of the story.

In my last few years in San Antonio we were on the itinerary of Chinese higher education representatives touring U. S. institutions as part of a State Department USAID educational exchange program. We were a new institution and had two faculty originally from China. We welcomed the delegation of faculty and administrators from different institutions from various mainland China locations, an interpreter, and someone from the State Department. We exchanged publications. Ours reflected our two-year technical and the two-year university transfer programs. Their publications focused on a single industry. The first delegation centered around everything railroads: engineers, designers, foodservice, mechanics, logistics, etc. It was completely foreign to us, but at the same time it made sense.

As we toured, the formality started to erode. Our reputation was made that first year when we went into the Student Center and entered the game room housing pool and ping-pong tables. There was a game going on, and I was greeted by the students, one of whom would face me in the end-of-term *Student Versus President Ping-Pong Challenge*. The interpreter described how that worked, and one of the Chinese presidents looked at me, smiled, and pointed to the table. I pointed to the table, and he nodded. We removed our jackets. I introduced the delegation to students and asked if we could have an impromptu game. They agreed and learned about ping-pong diplomacy and international relations, even if you couldn't speak the language. From that point the atmosphere changed. We toured the dance studio and ended up with a group picture of everyone, grinning ear to ear, toe-pointing at the ballet barres. They wanted copies to show the folks back home. That picture solidified Northeast Lakeview College for the next few years as a "must stop" for the annual exchange.

***

FILM (the *MOVIES*)

We were a generation entertained and educated by books and movies. One required attention and imagination, and the other offered lights, darkness, action, adventure, exotic locations, history, and the future brought to life. Movies compressed whole lives and historical periods, portrayed by the beautiful and the articulate, into two-hour slices of fanciful reality, readily available a few times per week for a nominal fee. Movies showed how we should behave. They taught history and those who peopled that history. Though movie versions of historical and current events were highly suspect, we benefited from the introduction to eras and significant players. The world was opened. Truth and accuracy would have to come later.

One of my favorite courses to teach was *Film as Literature,* operating under the assumption that most people, though influenced by movies, had little knowledge of their history, evolution, technology, and aesthetics. In essence, they were visually illiterate. It was my job to make them literate in sixteen weeks by showing milestone films that represented all they did not know. Films were chosen because of technological advances (from silent to talkies), films representing the best of a genre, films capturing a changing culture, and films reflecting the brilliance of a collaborative medium. I reminded students that a major appeal was the condensing and manipulation of time. By nature we are visual learners who needed to become discriminating viewers, ever on guard to evaluate and distinguish entertainment from reality.

I felt I had seen every movie made for the two years we were slowly destroyed by the *JET THEATER*, as we would frequently accompany our mother and work the refreshment stand and sweep up the candy wrappers, popcorn, and cigarette butts left by the twelve patrons in attendance. Many years later, after I had taken film coursework and began teaching film classes, I shared with my mother that I probably would not have developed an interest in film without our two-year ownership of the *JET*. She made it clear she did not believe the significant damage to the social and economic fabric of our family was an equal trade-off for the development of my academic versatility.

We all have favorite movies, and for reasons all personal. As a teacher of film I have two categories of "classics": those I appreciate for all the academic reasons, and those that speak to me personally. A colleague and I were swapping favorite movies, category by category. Al was a former Marine veteran wounded on his first day in Viet Nam. When we got to "scariest movies" I was sure he would laugh at my choice, *The Wizard of Oz*. I saw it at the age of six and had to walk the mile home at night with my older brother, convinced flying monkeys would appear at any moment and carry us back to the dungeon of the wicked witch. Al didn't laugh, but paused for a moment before voicing, *Bambi*. I assumed he was making fun of my choice until he shared that he lost his father at an early age. When he was very young he saw the movie and the scene where Bambi's mother is killed by hunters made it a terrifying experience.

January 10, 2016
Mr. Robert Osborne and Mr. Ben Mankiewicz
TURNER CLASSIC MOVIES
1050 Techwood Drive NW, Atlanta, GA 3031
Dear Mr. Osborne and Mr. Mankiewicz:

I want to thank all connected with the founding and flourishing of Turner Classic Movies (TCM). For many of us it is the major reason we pay monthly cable fees. It is not just that old/classic movies are featured; it is the quality of the production that surrounds each film. My purpose for writing is to suggest a category of people worthy of serving as "Guest Programmers." I would like to recommend film educators who have spent the last five decades, at least, sharing their passion for the movies; fighting academia (in the beginning) to convince decision-makers and colleagues that film was worthy of academic study; wrestling with the primitive technology needed to show feature length films; and dealing with the range of students (in the same classroom) who had never seen a silent film – to those who saw *Birth of a Nation* when it was released. Luckily, we were able to convince colleagues that movies were the major communication medium in the lives of students.

We have many stories to share about those early days when there was no TCM and, unless you lived in a major metropolitan area, a venue to view and discuss, older films. Examples of that wonderful time include:

- Waiting for cans of 16mm film to show up for the scheduled viewing. Nothing worse than facing a three-hour class without a two-hour movie.
- Managing a three-reel movie with ancient school projectors that were noisy, heavy, and notoriously fickle. I looked forward to presenting at outreach sites but dreaded the logistics of transporting equipment. My class met for three hours one night per week when no technical support was available. I brought scissors, tape, bulbs, and an extra projector into each class – and have more than once used a pencil and my finger in lieu of a functioning take-up reel to complete the viewing of a movie.
- Having to explain to young African American students, prior to the viewing, why *Birth of a Nation* was being shown and why it was considered a classic, of sorts.
- Refusing to teach on a small TV with the advent of videotape.

The first semester I taught Film as Literature at Broward Community College in Ft. Lauderdale, FL, was Fall 1974, which was when Siskel and Ebert debuted on TV and the American Film Institute (AFI) conferred the first Life Achievement Award to John Ford. As you can see from the attached flyers, it has been many years since I have taught a film course – but I could not keep away. In 2004 I decided to have a community film series, not knowing what kind of response we would get. I shouldn't have been surprised by the great response, as people from all over Denver came each week. I revived the series in San Antonio, TX, when we opened the new Performing Arts Center at the newest community college in the nation. I designed the new theater to include a large movie screen and a commercial Blu-ray projector. The response was the same. Despite the availability of TCM and Netflix, there are very few venues where people can see old movies on a large screen – and then discuss what they had just seen. Our *1st Tuesday* film series was dubbed "date night."

If anything confirmed the need to keep offering the series is the story of a gentleman who attended the Spring 2004 series in Colorado. The second movie screened was Howard Hawks' *Red River.* We had a great discussion, which was dominated by a man in his 50s who had been silent during the discussion of *Notorious* the week before. He braved a snowstorm to travel across town and would have stayed and talked about the movie all night. A few days later I received a postcard from him stating that he was a retired Marine and had been waiting years to have someone to talk to about his favorite movie. The night we discussed *Red River* was one of the highlights of his recent life.

Sincerely,

Dr. Eric Reno, Founding President (ret.)
Northeast Lakeview College
San Antonio, TX

* * *

March 3, 2004
Dr. Reno:

A word of appreciation for your efforts in the Red Rocks College [Lakewood, CO] film event. For years I have waited for an intelligent discussion on the classic, *Red River* of 1947-48.

Have thought about all that was said on Monday last. Your insights were of special note. I am aware of the responsibility you have for the entire "lash-up" of the institution. For you sir, to take the time and effort to share with those interested in classic films, your knowledge, time, and efforts is a genuine moment in never ending education for all concerned. I am certain "seniors" had thought stimulation for the entire evening of *Red River*. Pity the young people who do not realize what they are missing. They can never appreciate the value of, "Three cents, why that's more silver money than I have seen since the war."

Thank you, sir, for an enjoyable evening. Worth driving 20 miles in a snowstorm for. Great!

Respectfully
O. W. Ervin, USMC (Ret.)

There is a personal and meaningful backstory to Mr. Ervin's kind note of appreciation. Movies were not an important part of my father's life. I do not remember him attending or discussing movies he had seen, except for one unforgettable time that has marked generations of our family history. In 1948 he returned from a flight to Albuquerque, New Mexico, and said he had seen a movie we all had to see. I was six, my brother was eight, and my sister was three. That day he took us to the largest screen theater in Kansas City, and we became enthralled by the movie *Red River*. It became a family favorite we watch whenever the opportunity presents, scenes and dialogue memorized, our passion shared with our children.

We found out years later the film was considered a classic, one of the greatest westerns ever made. When

I taught film appreciation and designed my community film series I included *Red River* as a milestone film. One of the major characters is named Matthew Garth, played by Montgomery Clift. The main character is Thomas Dunson, played by John Wayne, in probably his finest performance. The film is ostensibly about the first cattle drive from Texas to Kansas following the Civil War, but as we discuss after the film has been shown, it is really about the love between father and son. My father had died by the time I had matured enough to discuss the how and whys of his love for that film. Pat and I named our first born after the Montgomery Clift character. His name is Matthew Blake Reno. He lived for thirty-two minutes. Nine years later we named our second child, Patrick Matthew Reno. He is aware of his name heritage.

My older brother, Alan, and wife, Fran, named their fourth son, Will, after the main character of Will Kane, played by Gary Cooper, from the classic western, *High Noon*. Will died too young, but his name and personality have been passed on to younger extended family members. Both the original Matt and Will are fictional characters, but they embodied qualities of character we wished upon our children.

During my third year in San Antonio one of our wonderful faculty, Dr. Dollie Hudspeth, submitted and received on behalf of the college a National Endowment for the Humanities (NEH) grant for a month-long series of community events related to the novel, *To Kill a Mockingbird*. Books were purchased and distributed, invitations printed and broadcast throughout the community, local and national speakers were scheduled, assignments were integrated into courses, workshops and presentations were scheduled in multiple venues. The kick-off event was a reception and presentation by Charles Shields, author of his recently published book, *A Portrait of Harper Lee.*

I hosted a showing and discussion of the award-winning film that captured a book-to-film-migration as well as any in the history of movies. We were joined that evening by Mary Badham, who played the role of Scout, the youngest character, whose innocence is the lens through which the story is told. Mary told wonderful behind-the-scenes stories about the making of the film and the life-long relationships amongst many of the cast. Mary and Gregory Peck, who played the character of her father, Atticus Finch – a Lincolnesque character, were close and kept in touch until his death. She always referred to Peck as "Atticus." From her perspective, the character of the actor was the character of the person he portrayed. The audience was enthralled by her stories and had questions that would have taken us into late night.

Pat and I offered to take Mary back to her hotel, but instead the three of us found a steakhouse, and fueled by food and drink, heard additional stories of the film and its participants. We also learned her husband was a community college administrator. Pat and I posed questions we believed reflected the impact of the book and its cinematic partner have had on the fabric of American culture.

Endearments are those public and private descriptors used to portray the closeness of a relationship. Some are casual and some are intended only for the other. Dear, Darling, Honey, Love of My Life, and more creative and intimate descriptors are always welcomed. But none ever matched what Pat told me many years ago. Out of nowhere she said I was her Atticus. Oh, the weight of an impossible responsibility!

14. JAZZ, JESUS, and OTHER COMMONALITIES

The relationship between fathers and sons is never neutral, but always life-lasting. My life is bound by two men I never got to know. Our first child lived for 32 minutes, and I lost my father for eight years. There was a part of me hoping this exercise would help to heal the hurts and right the wrongs. My father's death in 1962 made moot the great unanswered question as to what would have happened when my father and mother came to England in 1963, a trip they planned when I got my Air Force assignment in 1961. My father and I had hurt each other in ways that were deep and petty. I blamed him for my empty adolescence. I then looked forward to the things we could talk about if he had lived long enough to benefit from my developing maturity and compassion. I looked forward to talking about his love of music, which he passed on to me; his strong and private faith; his life, which we never discussed; my future and confusion.

When all was well with our family our parents had an addition built onto the back of our house in Kansas. On the first floor was a screened porch and on the second was the master bedroom, with the back and sides framed by floor to ceiling windows. Dubbed the "New Room," the bed was centered, and a baby grand piano stood in the corner overlooking the large pasture behind our house. Our father lived there. We were exposed to music our whole lives.

Six years later, when we moved to Florida, everything was sold. We were starting over. No piano, only a small portable record player to play the few albums that remained. A description of what was sold and what was kept would accurately reflect our financial situation. A year later our mother worked extra hours and surprised our father with a small electric piano. We were all old enough to know the significance of the gift. He sat down and could usually be found there.

I have imagined how our tentative adult relationship might have gone. I would have begun with jazz, his secondary passion to aviation. But why jazz? Because jazz was my father - complicated and private, internally soulful. Jazz is a large umbrella, absorbing cultural and generational influences; the varying, yet recognizable and exploratory; the lyrical and the explosive. I saw it as the music of sophistication and depth. It was where I wanted to be. I grew into it. My adolescence paralleled the beginning of commercial rock-n-roll, but I didn't become a fan for another decade. I had no classmates to talk to about jazz. I was out of musical step. I had never had a discussion with my father about his musical background and interests, except for one surprising incident.

When I was sixteen my father came into my room and handed me an album with the picture of Julian

"Cannonball" Adderley on the cover. Adderley had taught music at the "colored" high school in Fort Lauderdale and later would become a world-renowned jazz musician (alto sax). My father said: "I thought you might like to have this." I thanked him and proceeded to drive my family crazy over the next week playing the record at all opportunities. I do not know where he got the album and didn't realize he was aware of my interest, and we never talked about it. I couldn't wait to share jazz stories when they came to England.

I would have started with a story about Carmen McRae, the great jazz vocalist. When I worked for United Airlines in San Francisco in the late 1960s and early 1970s, the administrative offices were on Union Square. Late one afternoon an attractive, but obviously weary African American woman walked in and came to the counter. She took a deep breath, avoided my gaze, and said: "I need two tickets to L.A." I responded: "And what is the other name?" She quickly looked up, gave me a broad smile and said: "So, you know who I am." I knew Carmen McRae had been performing in North Beach to wonderful reviews. "I am a big fan." We spent the next fifteen minutes talking about her engagement, *The City*, jazz in general, and the great pleasure I had in meeting her. She said she expected me to attend her next visit and to sit down close. The meeting made both of our days.

Then I would share my piano stories, hoping they would lead to the relationship we never had. At *UAL* I struck up a friendship with the display manager who was responsible for glorifying the services and destinations of the airline. Basil Johns and I discovered we were jazz buffs and began trading albums. The summer of 1971 was the inaugural Concord Jazz Festival, featuring the Dave Brubeck Quartet, George Shearing, and Herbie Mann. Basil asked if we were going, and I said we wouldn't miss it. Dave Brubeck was born in Concord and Basil lived in Concord. He said he would be looking for us at intermission.

Thousands of fans were camped out with their blankets and picnic baskets, but Basil was able to find us at intermission. He was wearing a flowered short sleeve Hawaiian shirt I could have spotted a mile away. He invited us to his house after the concert. He said: "Dave will be there." I said: "Dave?" He replied, with a large smile: "Dave Brubeck and his family. Dave was born in Concord. We've been friends for twenty years and always try to get together to celebrate his wife's birthday." I said we would love to come over. Pat said she had never seen me so quiet. I just listened to stories about music and musicians. I was finally able to tell Mr. Brubeck I had seen him at the Royal Festival Hall in London in 1964, and that my airline pilot father played piano and, in the 1940s and 1950s, went to New York when he wanted a month of music. On occasion he would mention a blind piano player that he always went to see. It wasn't until years later when we guessed he was referring to Art Tatum, considered by many to be the greatest pianist in the history of jazz. I was thankful to be able to contribute something to the evening and silently thanked my father for my musical IQ.

I would have also told him how my musical history and interests helped me professionally. When I assumed my first presidency at Red Rocks Community College. I was following a beloved president, Dr. Dorothy Horrell, who was going to become the President of the state system of community colleges, and my new boss. My first official function as the new president was a black-tie holiday gala sponsored by the communities the college served. It took place a week prior to my report date, and I knew it was more than a social event for many; for some it was a community assessment of Dorothy's replacement. My new assistant sent me names and titles of key people I would need to get to know. It was an hour's drive to the event, and Pat quizzed me the whole time on names and positions of dignitaries I might encounter. My correct pairing of names and offices bordered on 50% by the time we arrived. But I survived the reception, and we were called into dinner.

The seating arrangements were programmed. Pat and I were seated next to Dan Leach and his wife, Sherry. Dan was the Chair of the Presidential Search Committee, who had made it obvious he didn't want Dorothy to leave. I was the chosen replacement, but it seemed he had more investigating to do. We got into small talk, and he asked what I liked to do outside of my professional responsibilities. I told him I liked to read, attend my children's activities, loved old movies, and, that I was a jazz buff. I saw an immediate physical shift but wasn't sure what it meant. He looked at me and asked: "What instruments are you a fan of?" I told him I was partial to jazz guitar and piano. He focused even more intently. "Who are your favorite pianists?" This wasn't an idle question. "Well, I like Brubeck and Peterson, but my favorite is Bill Evans." He gave me an even more intense stare and asked questions to make sure I hadn't been prepped, and to see what I knew about Bill Evans.

I passed the test and learned that as a teenager he had received a Bill Evans youth scholarship. Dan was a jazz pianist himself, and Bill Evans was his favorite. We became good friends. I enjoyed his company and support for my whole term at Red Rocks. This interaction is an example of how often interests and awareness outside of professional responsibilities help to build friendships and navigate situations that can determine success or failure somewhere down the road.

I clinched the budding relationship by telling him of the time when Pat and I were living in San Francisco and read that Evans was appearing at a club in North Beach. I was working half-time at United and going to graduate school. We didn't have much money and checked our budget – just enough if we nursed our drinks. We had a memorable, yet thirsty, evening. The next day at school I went into the cafeteria and saw posted signs announcing: "Bill Evans will be lecturing and performing at the music theater. Free for all registered students." I would also share with my father my involvement in the Denver Jazz on Film Festival, presenting on a panel and discussing "Does Film Do Justice to Jazz?"

What I dreamed about most was a surprise visit to Ronnie Scott's Jazz Club, the place where the greats performed. I knew it had been many years since my father had experienced live music. I envisioned us sitting at a small table, ordering a beer, listening to the music, not saying a word, hoping the venue would serve as balm on our maturing relationship.

Then it would be my father's turn, and I was sure hidden similarities would have surfaced. I would ask him about the origin of his musical interests. I would be curious about the Reno Brothers, who played locally at small towns in Michigan – where, what, and how often? Uncle Phil (two years older) loved the audience. He would become the musical Mayor of Wayland, Michigan. The image I had for my father was of someone sitting in the dark corner of a bar, smoke rising from behind the piano, a beer within reach, and a solitary pianist picking out notes to a tune that would slowly reveal itself.

I would have been eager to hear stories of his years of flying into New York. He would have been in NYC at the height of the jazz world's popularity. I hoped to hear about venues and vocal and instrumental voices. I would have brought up names out of the jazz *Who's Who*. Just as I loved my solitary exploration of London, I imagined my father visiting jazz clubs on his own because I never saw or heard him discussing or sharing his stories with another person. I wanted to be that person who shared his passion, and the audience for his stories, but it was too late.

Then we would get specific and share artists and songs, sharing a beer, and becoming friends. I still fantasize about our father and son discovery of common interests, and what might have led to the relationship I had missed.

* * *

The more I reflect and the more I write, the more I see my father in who I became. We were not joiners. We were members of professional organizations but never members of voluntary organizations. Neither of us wanted to be identified by those who could claim our loyalty, our beliefs, our character. I attempt to avoid descriptive one and two-word labels that make lazy assumptions. I never knew the political affiliation of our parents. I knew only their values.

The final decade of our father's life was void of close friends and acquaintances. He was liked and respected by colleagues but never sought out social relationships. The friends he had were from the early aviation years. Our mother was the social magnet. She quickly made friends, but rarely were they a major part of our lives.

My adolescence established lifelong behaviors I hadn't connected. I never had "buddies," friends that are forever in your life, and with whom you communicate regularly and schedule annual events. I did not terminate relationships; others would take their place. I love the company of people and have wonderful friendships, but they are usually isolated by time and place. I have led mini-lives, bordered by a physical distancing and a psychological solitude I have lived with since those early years.

I am an old-fashioned mid-western Christian, characterized by being church-going, God-fearing, and Golden-Rule following. I read the book and do my best to follow its teachings. I want religion to be a comfort and spiritual guide. I want to rely on my faith, but the longer I live the less comfort I experience. I believe in a religion and a savior who teach and expect those teachings to be applied. I do not expect a prescriptive God who endows us with qualities but forbids us to use what we have been given. I want to be a child of God, not a puppet.

When I was young I ended my prayers by asking God that, if someone had to die, "Please let it be me or Dad." It was a practical request: my death would protect everyone I loved, and I would avoid the trauma of loss and grief. I offered our father because he had a full and memorable beginning, but physical damage had taken away much of what he loved in life, with little chance it could ever be regained. This shallow logic clearly defines "hubris" long before I had any understanding of Greek tragedy.

My father read and thought, occasionally sharing an insight into his faith, affecting me to a greater degree than any sermons. He never preached. As an adult he didn't attended church, but recounted visiting heaven in a near-death medical emergency. Though there were no trappings of faith, he may have been the most spiritual person I have known. If he had lived until the planned England trip, I had hoped we would talk, and I would gain substance for my tenants of faith. To the extent of our spiritual relationship, his is the model I have followed. His relationship was with God. He did not require an interpreter, but I would have valued what he wanted to share.

In the 1950s, TV programming usually ended at midnight. My pilot brother and I usually watched the sign-off of one of the three stations – a beautifully framed film of a F86 *Sabre Jet* searching the sky for the majesty of faith, with the reading of the aviator's powerfully poetic hymn, "High Flight," by a voice of heaven narrator in the background, ending with the jet hurtling skyward.

HIGH FLIGHT

Oh! I have slipped the surly bonds of earth
And danced the skies on laughter-silvered wings;
Sunward I've climbed and joined the tumbling mirth
Of sun-split clouds - and done a hundred things
You have not dreamed of - wheeled and soared and swung
High in the sunlit silence. Hovering there,
I've chased the shouting wind along, and flung
My eager craft through footless halls of air.
Up, up the long, delirious, burning blue
I've topped the wind-swept heights with easy grace
Where never lark, or even eagle flew -
And, while with silent lifting mind I've trod
The high untrespassed sanctity of space,
Put out my hand and touched the face of God.

- John Gillespie Magee Jr.

It is a celebration. It portrays the joyful integration of the temporal world we inhabit and the heaven we strive to deserve. The poem reflects our father's life and passion, and the faith he so privately held. His influence has never left me.

15. DISCRIMINATION and OTHER DIFFERENCES

Race and its adjunct social issues influence all who have lived in our country. I have straddled the border of segregation and integration and hated that my country hasn't been able to shed the myths that have poisoned our promise and our national character. But I was born into the national complicity of prejudice and discrimination. Some prejudices took years, and even decades to overcome. Some citizens retain forever what they were born into.

I share the following interactions for no reason other than they were educational, memorable, and illustrative. When we moved to Florida in 1954 I entered my first segregated school district and *Brown v. the Board of Education* was heard by the Supreme Court. The Court's unanimous decision to outlaw "separate but equal" education became the law of the land, even though it took a decade to see its implementation. I was in the Air Force in England on August 28,1963, when the March on Washington took place. It was a few months past my 21st birthday and my designation as a full-fledged adult citizen of the United States.

I was now eligible to vote, a right denied many fellow citizens of the same age, but of a different color. I was in London the weekend following the March when a man in his 40s, well dressed, goatee, and plaid vest, ran up to me, grabbed my arm and shouted: "You have to stop them!" He obviously knew I was an American. "Stop who?" "Didn't you see what they did in Washington? If you don't stop them they will be doing it here." I lifted his hand off my arm and gave him a look I hoped expressed what I was thinking. America was not the only country with a problem.

In the Spring of 1975, Maya Angelou spent a week on the North Campus of Broward Community College. We were the newest and smallest campus of the college and having her for a week put us on the educational map. No one could have been more gracious and down-to-earth. She made presentations, sat in on classes, was available in informal settings. She was more than a visitor. We learned about "sheroes" and argued about whether William Faulkner was a racist. Differing points of view were heated but civil. Facts and examples supported opinion. Opinions may not have been completely changed, but they were altered. Our discussions were education at its best. Everyone with whom she came in contact knew they were in the presence of greatness and grace.

At the end of the week the English Dept. had a going away party, hosted by Dr. Shelby Lee, who had invited her to campus. The beer and wine flowed, and our admiration continued to grow. That year a colleague and I vowed to meet regularly to critique each other's writings. There were no writings to date; thus, no meetings. We named ourselves the Non-Writers Literary Guild and declared Maya Angelou the first woman and first honorary member to be admitted to our organization. Her publications barred her from achieving full standing. The membership certificate was presented. Her acceptance speech was memorable, though no one remembers exactly what was said. One of our treasures is an inscribed copy of *I Know Why the Caged Bird Sings.*

One year in the 1980s, Broward Community College hosted a MLK celebration dinner, and I was fortunate enough to be seated at the table of the keynote spear, Mr. Julian Bond, President of the NAACP. In addition to his history of commitment and dedication in the struggle for civil rights, he was also known as one of the most eloquent speakers in the country. The combined qualities of his voice, the delivery, and the content kept audiences in the palm of his hand. I was still wrestling with lifelong stage fright. I told him how much I admired his public speaking skills and wondered if it was a natural gift or something he worked hard on. He then surprised the whole table by saying that into his adult years he had stage fright and was terrified of public speaking. He saw a therapist who asked if he drank alcohol, and he replied he liked an occasional glass of wine. The therapist recommended that he have a glass of wine one-half hour before speaking. He took his advice and had not had a problem since.

The most problematic of my savored memories occurred in the United Airlines San Francisco office, directly across the street from the St. Francis Hotel, where Presidents stayed. One day in 1970, a grim African American man came to the counter. He wanted a ticket to Los Angeles. He was dressed in a uniform, stating an organization's name I did not recognize. He invited no conversation, glared and paid. I saw him weekly, and he always waited until I was available. "Good afternoon" was finally acknowledged, and I asked about his organization. He indicated it was a militant organization willing to go to any lengths to right the wrongs of discrimination, even committing acts of violence against good people like myself if necessary. It couldn't be helped. I was honored to be designated as a "good person." He continued to wait for me. We would have brief conversations, and I hoped his attitude might change. After a few months I never saw him again and wondered what happened and how he lived the remainder of his life. For a few moments I even wondered if we might have become friends.

I grew up with the black-white issue, and it wasn't until I moved to Colorado that I became aware of the depth of the brown-white injustices. The "No Dogs or Mexicans Allowed" signage had once been common, the tried-and-true method of dehumanizing the largest minority in the United States and establishing an identifiable scapegoat for the ills of our country. Though the depth of their treatment as an American minority has yet to become mainstream history, the treatment of Asian immigrants followed in unique, horrific, and universal ways. Our understanding of what happened to Japanese Americans in WWII is the exception.

That anti-Semitism continues within the memory of a recent world war that murdered millions of innocent men, women, and children is disheartening. That having a different religion, being of a different race, faith or gender, and having a different sexual orientation are enough to be considered "non-American" shames the foundation of our cherished democracy. What the injustices have in common is the existence of identifiable differences and measurable ignorance.

Sexual differences were the darkest of secrets for the first three decades of my life – never discussed, described, understood, always feared, and never acknowledged. There were occasional rumors in high school and the military, especially when classmates failed the FBI background investigation and were reassigned midway through our training as intelligence analysts. Being a homosexual meant a student was a prime candidate for being blackmailed, and giving away confidential information under duress. My introduction to the gay community took place in the late 1960s when I moved to San Francisco. Being openly gay was accepted, but it didn't guarantee equal standing in society.

The Downtown Terminal was in the basement of the Hilton Hotel where major airlines had counters and where buses brought people in from and back to the airport. It was not in the best part of town and opened at 6:00am. I worked at the main office on Union Square until I asked to work half-time so I could begin graduate school at San Francisco State University. My request was approved, but I was assigned to the Terminal. My scheduled changed: arise at 4:30am, walk a mile to the bus, board the streetcar, and walk from Market St., through the Tenderloin section of *The City*, just as the pimps and prostitutes were going to breakfast. Prior to my first day at my new assignment I imagined having the streetcar to myself. I was wrong; I had to stand all the way to downtown – discovering an early morning culture I had not been aware of.

During my time on Union Square I became acquainted with co-workers who never denied their sexual orientation. I also noticed they were eventually transferred to the Downtown Terminal. I reacquainted myself with many former co-workers after my transfer. After a few months I was asked by a colleague to come out to the center of the round terminal. Jack asked that I turn a complete circle and look at the counters of the many airlines, and the approximate twenty total employees. He said: "Eric. Guess what? You are the only straight guy here."

A few weeks later I mentioned to Jack I had purchased a new stereo system and wondered if he knew of anyone who might want my old system. He immediately said he was interested and asked if I could bring it to his apartment. I said no problem, that Pat and I would bring it over. Pat was extremely nervous, never knowingly having met a gay person. "What do I say? What can I say? How should I act?" In hindsight this tragic comedy had us scripted as meeting our first Martians, discussing the etiquette of interacting with our first extraterrestrials rather than fellow human beings we had been conditioned to fear. We were welcomed, met Jack's partner, Neil, a General

Practitioner, the wine and cheese were served, and we spent a thoroughly enjoyable evening admitting to and laughing about our innocent ignorance, and becoming friends.

October 27, 2020: REPAIRING the DAMAGE

The United States of America is a country of damaged values and damaged citizens. America became a damaged society in 1619 when the first slaves were delivered to Virginia. Many will rightly state that our treatment of Native Americans predates that by more than a century. We were a country that believed skin color was a determining factor in the assignment of social status, political participation, economic opportunities, and intellectual competency. The damage to those of a different color is well documented, and I will not repeat the history and catalog of heinous crimes inflicted on African Americans. I want to discuss the damage racism has done to the white majority, myself included.

I am a 4th generation middle class WASP and have never been socially, psychologically, economically, verbally, or physically abused because of my skin color. The first half of my childhood was in the heart of our country, the State of Kansas, where I was never a witness to racial discrimination. There was no one in our small community to discriminate against. We were of one color and a common heritage. At the onset of adolescence we moved to South Florida (1954) where discrimination was firmly entrenched: separate neighborhoods, schools, drinking fountains and bathrooms, beaches, seating in a variety of facilities, entertainment venues, and areas I am probably ignorant of to this day. We accepted the arrangements, but no one told us why they existed or why they were necessary.

When you have been raised in an environment of established values, their shattering and reformation are a process, rarely a revelation. In my new community school we were taught, directly and indirectly, that the Civil War was a romantic moment in our history, with the two sides representing the underdog chivalric South versus the mighty industrial North. The concept of "states' rights" was introduced as the main reason for the Civil War. It was not just about slavery. Under the microscope, if the concept of "states' rights" had prevailed, each state would have been allowed to continue enslaving the minds and bodies of fellow human beings. The *Declaration of Independence* and the *Constitution* would have become historical relics of a universal, but failed dream. Welcome to segregated America. I learned you didn't question; it had always been this way. Fortunately, we had parents who didn't accept segregation as a natural condition.

There is a prominent memory that served to educate us at an early age about the destructive practice of discrimination. We were fascinated by our father, the youngest licensed pilot in the State of Michigan in the 1920s. The lovingly designed albums kept by our mother followed his early professional career in the late 1930s as a pilot for *TWA*. In one scrapbook was a picture of a distinguished negro (the language of the era) standing in front of a *TWA* DC3, dressed in a uniform that would have done credit to *GQ* magazine, with the inscription: "To Max Reno. One of the best pilots I know. From Sid." Sid was a uniformed skycap, greeting passengers, checking luggage, and assisting where needed, but we never learned the origin or depth of their relationship, one that occupied a prominent location in the scrapbook and planted a subconscious understanding in the minds of his children completely foreign to the segregated South that was our new home.

At my father's funeral in 1962 we heard other stories that meshed principle and practice. He was walking through the airline terminal when he was approached by a "colored" gentleman who asked if he knew where he could get something to eat. My father pointed to the restaurant and the man stated he was not allowed to eat in there. My father told the man to join him in the restaurant. The waitress said she could not serve colored people, and my father said: "I'll have a hamburger and put whatever my friend wants on my check. We have a plane to catch."

Slowly the barriers started coming down. Laws, legislation, the growth of civil rights and community action made it possible to start the healing and the opening of possibilities. New generations did not face the formal structures of racism, but fear, stupidity, and ignorance continued to be carriers of the racist poison. As a recent grandparent I have become more aware of the behavior of infants and toddlers, their innocence and loss of innocence. Watching children playing without a seeming awareness of racial differences is a joyful experience, soon to be destroyed when those differences are pointed out. The preaching and modeling of racism and hate by adults and institutions is a deadly, tragic, and for many, a life-long form of child abuse. Most rise above the injustices of our society, but too many take comfort in having someone to blame, someone to hate.

I know I "wuz robbed" early in life. I will never know if I missed meeting a best friend, helpful colleague, good neighbor, professional advisor, civic leader, spiritual leader, mentor, soulmate, life's companion, or the hundreds of roles that emerge when communities embrace each other. I also missed out on the exposure to a rich and joyful culture that was strictly off limits.

Enough of the old racist history and behaviors remain that continue to damage our individual and collective humanity. We just need to listen and look around. It won't go away until we acknowledge that silence and passivity are forms of complicity. It is no longer just the responsibility of "officials" to legislate fairness. We all are responsible for teaching and modeling the humanity a great nation must embrace and reflect if it is ever to deserve the titles, "The Leader of the Free World" and being a "Christian Nation." We owe it to ourselves, especially our innocent children, and those who once admired what we stood for.

Eric Reno

16. RECOGNITION and AFFIRMATION

The gift of giving back.

We all bear a degree of responsibility for the life we have led and the person we have become, but we can know ourselves only so well. We need the assistance of others who know and observe us. I was blessed six months into my second year of teaching. Dr. Max Raines, Distinguished Professor of Higher Education from Michigan State University, and national figure on community colleges, spent a semester at the college, visiting campuses, holding meetings, sitting in on gatherings, and making recommendations. We struck up an acquaintance due to common Michigan backgrounds and found we had other areas of interest: tennis and jazz. One day at lunch we were discussing my background and professional aspirations. He listened and then asked me about becoming a college president. If a feather had been handy you could have knocked me ten yards out of my chair. I laughed, but he added: "You can be a president if you want." I have never forgotten what he said. I have never forgotten that he said it.

A leader has the responsibility to affirm, support, and recognize. It goes with the title, as do many recognitions and awards – some deserved and some ceremonial. Those that have meaning are truly valued: presented by students, from colleagues and employees, and those where mettle reflects the substance of the medal. The *Colorado Community College President of the Year* awards, as chosen by students, stand at the top of the list. A concluding recognition was being honored in April 2022 when the Northeast Lakeview College art gallery was named the *Reno Gallery*, in recognition of a commitment to the arts. I was proud of our collective efforts, in programming and facilities, and accepted the honor with joy and gratitude.

I received tremendous satisfaction in watching and assisting in the growth of students and employees. When Northeast Lakeview College opened I continued the practice I had begun at Red Rocks CC: thirty minutes with the President. Within the first semester of being hired, all new fulltime employees were required to schedule a half hour with the President. They already knew me from the first meeting of a semester-long orientation program. Some were excited, and some were terrified. Seeing a scheduled thirty minutes on my calendar made my day. When they came into the office they usually sat in a chair across from my desk. I told them we were going to sit in the two guest chairs that were adjacent.

Excited and terrified initial responses were always the same. They would tell me about their job at the College. I would stop them and let them know I was aware of what they did. "Tell me about yourself, your family, your hopes, and your professional aspirations." From that point on we always had a wonderful time, discovering commonalities, and usually going past the thirty minutes. The time was about them, but they learned about me. They learned I wasn't born a college president, that I was an "accidental educator." My assistant knew not to schedule anything until at least forty-five minutes past our starting point. It was a simple, yet significant and enjoyable practice in building a culture.

I also ensured that faculty, staff, and students were provided with professional development opportunities that would expand their understanding of the greater mission of the college. I took a few faculty every year to an international education conference in Washington, D.C. On the final day of our first trip, one of our outstanding faculty, Prof. Cuihua Zhang, asked if she could be excused from the final sessions so she could see historic sites prior to our afternoon departure. Cuihua had come to America from China, and this was her first visit to our nation's capital. I approved, and she set a sightseeing record. From that point on I made it policy that, if possible, anyone going to a conference should book travel arrangements arriving a day ahead and returning a day following so they could explore the location they had been visiting. Those extra days come under the category of "professional development."

I attempted to practice "Distributive Leadership." Presidents get more invitations to professional and community events than they could possibly attend. But they could be represented. I was judicious in ensuring the institution was there, and represented by a proud, beaming, and prepped employee. We established college committees that everyone had the opportunity to be a member of, including the opportunity to chair or co-chair. Employees were treated as educators with different responsibilities. The favorite committees were *Professional Development* and *Celebrations and Rituals.*

My favorite tradition was the establishment of NLC's *First Friday* meeting. Educational institutions have faculty meetings. NLC had college meetings, attendance required of all employees. A documented absence was required. When? 2:00-3:00pm the first Friday of each month. The time and day are probably seen as attendance killers. I have seen institutions where employees believed such meetings were optional. First Friday worked because it was part of the developing culture. The meeting had rotational chairs and co-chairs from across the employee spectrum. It was a time of welcomes, goodbyes, announcements, and streamlined presentations – a two-hour agenda, once a month, compressed into an hour meeting. People arrived early, knowing they were going to see colleagues and stayed after to visit. We were a family of professionals.

In some ways my inferiority complex never left me. I felt uncomfortable being called "Dr. Reno," having a difficult time acknowledging an accomplishment beyond what was once believed possible. During my first presidency at Red Rocks Community College I was "Eric," and that informality worked. I was comfortable with that and so was everyone else. At my next and last presidency, in San Antonio, everyone insisted on calling me "Dr. Reno." It was important to them; they valued the formality and wanted outsiders to know their leader was a "Doctor." They didn't want to diminish who I was, nor the institution I represented. I would frustrate my family when I introduced myself to someone I had just met as "being in community colleges," and that I was building one from the ground up. My daughters would say: "Dad, why don't you tell them you are the President? They probably think you are in construction." It was also important to them for people to know who their father was.

It was also important that students and employees were recognized and encouraged by the President. I represented the office; the office had meaning and significance. I was just the current occupant. That is why the institutional culture was as important as the physical entity. The setting and facilities remain, but the people change. "We are all temporary stewards." For a culture to flourish and grow it must be taught, embraced, and modeled.

I had the best job in the world. I watched students and employees grow. I saw past failures return to school and become academic and social successes, changed by life experience and maturity. Being in a leadership position is a sacred trust, creating an environment where personal growth is encouraged, promoted, recognized, and rewarded. It is an obligation we owe those who did the same for us.

At every graduation ceremony a *Spirit of NLC* recipient is announced. Winners represent the employee spectrum – nominated by anyone and determined by a committee of previous recipients and college leaders. The large and beautiful crystal award is a proud and prized possession. It represents being noticed and appreciated for living the institutional values every day. I am a proud honorary recipient.

Epilogue

> "We are all of us born with a letter inside us, and that only if we are true to ourselves, may we be allowed to read it before we die." - Douglas Coupland

There are no sermons in this memoir, only the memories of the person who lived it. The stories reflect the universal moments of innocence and ignorance, stupidity and maturation, failures and accomplishments. As the ingested hormones flash through my body seeking to stem the lurking cancer, I listed the questions I should have asked, the answers I should have shared, and the advice I should have taken.

I hope readers were entertained, possibly enlightened, and permanently reminded of the gift of life and the responsibility to be thoughtful and active stewards of the journey. I will miss the big and small of life: beginning the morning in search of the perfect donut, the company of family and friends, the people I haven't met, the redeeming mystery of human creativity – the music, art, written and spoken words that explore, reveal, and celebrate the human condition.

We have a family reunion every two years: a gathering of 40-50 siblings, grand/great parents, spouses, aunts and uncles, sons, daughters, in-laws, cousins, nephews, nieces, and significant others. My older brother and I have had many discussions concerning how little we really knew about the lives of our parents – why certain events happened. We decided, as the family elders, to devote one evening to an open forum on family histories, shared insights only we possessed, and answered questions from anyone about anything. Then, as we listed our family history of surprises, successes, mistakes, poor choices, and missed opportunities, it hit me. I looked around the room at the beautiful faces of those we loved and realized that if life had worked out to our design, more than half of the people in the room would never have been born.

I will miss not knowing what became of my family. I fear for their futures, laboring under the assumption of having the power to influence and protect their lives. My only hope is the existence of that afterlife that connects the temporal with the eternal, or the fact I may have added value to their lives that will protect them. I want to be that specter that resides in the frontal lobe or back of the brain that asks the question, when a moral or ethical dilemma presents itself: "What would Dad/Grandpa/Eric/Uncle Rick/Dr. Reno do?" But the greater hope is they will be able to provide the answers for themselves.

Those we love, know, and affect deserve the best of us. I want to be memorable to those I have known, loved, and worked with. Not for reasons of vanity, but because of something I said, a kindness shown, a behavior they admired, an affirmation of their actions, encouragement towards a goal, praise for an accomplishment, a way of looking at an issue never considered, tending to a hurt, forgiveness for an unintended slight, smiling for no apparent reason.

My proofing reveals a smaller life than the one imagined. But it is a life, and I tried my best, with the good sense to seek help and advice from the best of the living and the dead. I am the eternal editor of my thoughts and form. I am a better judge of what I have written than what I have written. I could have said it better or not at all. Insights present themselves and change in significance as a product of the writing process. This is not a complete life narrative. I have done my best to be as truthful as memory allows, but I have done stupid and hurtful things through actions of omission and commission. Those rites provided hard-earned lessons I would have preferred to avoid.

In closing, I hope the narrative revealed a progression of awareness and maturity, and that the disjointed pieces eventually formed a coherent whole. I would like to bring in my 19th Century traveling companion, Mr. Charles Dickens, for a comforting closing perspective: "Happiness is a gift and the trick is not to expect it, but to delight in it when it comes." (***Nicholas Nickleby***)

ADDENDUM

Upon Retirement

"Dr. Reno: Thank you for the many opportunities you have given me, pushing me above and beyond the potential I didn't realize I had."

"Dr. Reno: You returned to Texas in 2004 to get a new college built, hire faculty and staff, and fill classrooms. In the meantime you created a lasting culture which values personal engagement and academic excellence. Your leadership also built the leader in me. You are truly an inspiration."

"Dear Dr. Reno: As I sit down to write this, I find myself at a loss for the words to express what you mean to me as a faculty member of NLC (Northeast Lakeview College). I have been here three years, but in that time I have been able to learn by watching you be the type of President that has the best interests of all in mind as you do the job."

"Dear Dr. Reno: what can I say but 'Thank You' and you will be missed terribly. You have been the glue that has held us together and the inspiration for all NLC has accomplished. From the first day I met you in 2006, I remember how impressed I was that you had read my resume and asked me about one of my presentations on the film, *The Quiet Man*. This attention to detail is evident in all you do, and I have personally appreciated it all the way from making this a beautiful campus to knowing details about faculty, staff, and students. Your legacy will continue as you have created a culture of inclusion and open doors."

"Dr. Reno: The dynamic culture you created at NLC is a positive reflection of your inclusive leadership style. I was so impressed (and nervous) about our 30 minute meeting – you were great and I had great hopes for the future. . . . By investing in your employees you have left part of your soul behind in each of us. . . . I will continue to see NLC through your eyes – as if anything is possible. It was an honor to serve as one of your founding faculty members."

"I've always enjoyed working with Dr. Reno. I've never encountered a person who is so open to new ideas and has the motivation to make them happen."

"Dr. Reno: It has been my profound pleasure to have met you. You have been an outstanding influence on me. Your conversations, advice and counsel have been most appreciated. . . . Thank you for coming into my life."

"Dear Dr. Reno: Thank you for welcoming me to NLC. The 30 minute meetings with new employees (often going longer) really set the tone for working at NLC. Thanks for taking the time to get to know me and your employees."

"Dr. Reno: You are an inspiration. Building a culture which reflects your values and leadership make it a real treat to come to work. . . . Thank you for rekindling my love for classic movies. Know when Gene Kelly dances and sings – to me it's you!"

"Dr. Reno: As cool as it is to say I know the President of the college, it's even cooler to say he knows me by name as well. Thanks for ALWAYS making each and everyone feel included. You may be leaving but you will always be here."

The Works

What follows are influences in the skilled hands of creative people who shine the light on universal moments of our lives, affecting us singularly. My notes do not reflect accepted critical interpretation. They belong to me. They give form to feelings I couldn't express. Be my guest: backtrack and identify those meaningful external influences in your life. Create your own categories and list those moments that have helped give an understanding of all you have observed, all you have become.

Music

- "Blame It On My Youth" (Kenny Rankin) & "Why Did I Choose You?" (Freddy Cole): The wrenching emotions of lost first love, followed by the joy of finding "The One."
- "I Can't Make You Love Me": A painfully beautiful song of loss. (Bonnie Raitt)
- "Our Love is Here to Stay": Our song. Every couple needs "their song."
- "Peace Piece": Get comfortable and listen for the next 6 minutes and 32 seconds. Deep and

comforting thoughts are soon to follow. (Bill Evans)

- "What's Going On" & "Mercy, Mercy Me": The soulful tandem that will make you want to lay down your gun, ask forgiveness from those you have wronged, and begin to clean up your life and the environment. (Marvin Gaye)
- "Amazing Grace": A transformative Spiritual.
- "Rhapsody in Blue" (George Gershwin) & "Appalachian Spring" (Aaron Copland): Classical Americana's musical portrait of our country's beauty, energy, character, and promise.
- "Wildfire" (Michael Martin Murphey): A haunting musical myth of America's historical heartland.

Short Stories

- "The Eighty-Yard Run": Life is a marathon, not a sprint. (Irwin Shaw)
- "Gold Coast": Be careful who you pretend to be. (James Alan McPherson)
- "Sonny's Blues": The meaningful responsibility of being your brother's/sister's keeper. (James Baldwin)

Novels

- *An Appointment in Samara*: What goes around comes around. (John O'Hara)
- *Lie Down in Darkness*: Feeling the hellish world of mental illness. (William Styron)

- *Under the Volcano*: Feeling the hellish world of alcoholism. (Malcolm Cowley)
- *The Alexandria Quartet*: Learning that what we think we know, seen through the eyes of others, brings into question our own judgment. (Lawrence Durrell)
- *Losing Battles*: The complexity and the humanity in the simplicity. (Eudora Welty)
- *The Great Gatsby*: The American Dream. Having the ability and resources to remake who we are. (F. Scott Fitzgerald)
- *Lord Jim*: Restoring personal integrity, even at the cost of our life. (Joseph Conrad)
- *Zen and the Art of Motorcycle Maintenance*: It's the journey, not the destination. (Robert Pirsig)
- *Billy Budd*: The inability to communicate often results in violence as a final form of expression. (Herman Melville)
- *Four Treasures of the Sky*: What we neglected to learn about the early Chinese experience in America. (Jenny Tinghui Zhang)

Non-Fiction

- The *Bible:* More effective as a guide than as a club.
- *The Fire Next Time*: My introduction to the history, complexity, and cruelty of American racism. (James Baldwin)
- *Seven Pillars of Wisdom*: No one says it better than Lawrence of Arabia: "All men dream: but not equally. Those who dream by night in the dusty

recesses of their minds wake up in the day to find it was vanity, but the dreamers of the day are dangerous men, for they may act their dreams with open eyes, to make it possible." (T. E. Lawrence)

Poetry

- "The Bee": What we would do to protect the ones we love. (James Dickey)

Drama

- *Death of a Salesman*: A cautionary tale of losing the person you are and could have become. (Arthur Miller)

Film

- *It's a Wonderful Life*: The measure of a life, rarely asked. (Frank Capra)
- *Citizen Kane*: Genius portrayal of a flawed genius. (Orson Welles)
- *The Best Years of Our Lives*: A perfect movie capturing the humanity of psychological and physical recovery after WWII. It improves with each viewing. (William Wyler)
- *Odd Man* Out: My favorite movie. Beautifully compelling tragedy. Must be watched in the dark, with no interruptions or distractions. Preferably with a glass of wine and two hours set-aside for recovery and discussion (Sir Carol Reed)

Acknowledgments

My sincere thanks to Lee Reno, whose insistence that I read Grandma Mae Reno's daily diaries after a thirty-year hiatus was the catalyst for all that followed.

To Rick Busch, whose fifty-five years as mentor and friend, and initial critic and enthusiastic supporter, kept me at the keyboard.

To Dr. Christina Minihan, neighbor, professional colleague, and friend, for her insights and advice concerning the formidable world of publications.

The book would never have been completed without the welcoming support of those I met at THE **WRITING** CONSULTANCY. I was welcomed and guided by Keirsten Clark, expertly shepherded into organization and content by Jon Curzon, and held accountable for my structure and mechanics by Neil Broadfoot. They were generous in their praise and diplomatic and "on point" in their constructive criticism.

My eternal thanks to Sarah Shriber, my *Author Manager*, for her responsiveness, recommendations, and cautions. She responded to my many questions and changes with good humor and solid advice.

About the Author

Dr. Eric Reno is a child of the American Midwest, armed with its accompanying values. He served four years in the United States Air Force and attended the Junior College of Broward County, FL; Florida Atlantic University; and San Francisco State University. He was twice named by students Colorado Community College President of the Year. He received the Shirley B. Gordon Award of Distinction from Phi Theta Kappa (PTK), the international honor society of two-year colleges. In 2011 he was named Honorary Commander of the 435th Fighter Training Squadron at Randolph AFB. In 2013 he received the Hidalgo recognition from the Bexar County (San Antonio) Commissioners' Court. In 2014 he was named to the PTK Texas Hall of Honor for distinguished CEOs and received the Michael Bennett Lifetime Achievement Award. In 2014 he received the National Pacesetter Award from the National Council for Marketing and Public Relations (NCMPR), recognizing his advocacy on behalf of two-year colleges. In 2022 Northeast Lakeview College honored his support of the arts by naming the art gallery the RENO GALLERY.

Eric and Patricia reside in Fort Collins, CO, with their children and grandchildren all within commuting distance.

END-OF-BOOK PHOTOS

15. Eric and Patricia: Newlyweds – 1968

16. Mothers' Day, 1995

THE CHRONICLE

of Higher Education

MONEY & MANAGEMENT

'Building a Culture'

Community-college campuses of the future emphasize convenience and flexibility

17. *Chronicle of Higher Education*: "Building a Culture" – 2006

18. NLC Founding VPs – Dr. Beth Lewis (Academics), Dr. Debbie Hamilton (Students), Dr. Tangila Dove (Business) – 2008

19. Pat and flight trainer, Tony: Spouse Taxi, Randolph AFB – 2011
"Don't touch anything!"

20. *President's 1st Tuesday Community Film Series:* 2008-2013

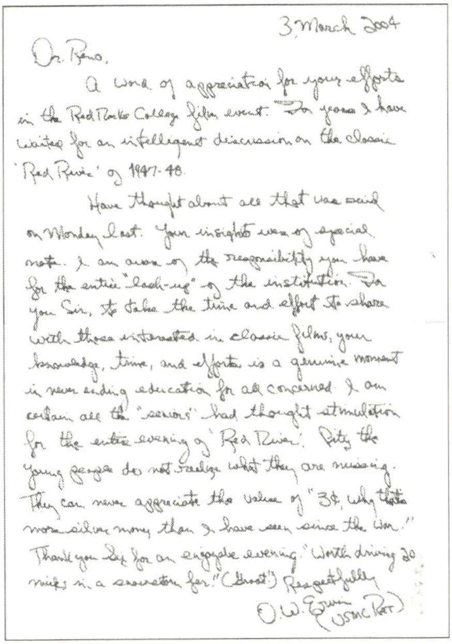

3 March 2004

Dr. Reno,

A word of appreciation for your efforts in the Red Rocks College film event. For years I have waited for an intelligent discussion on the classic 'Red River' of 1947-48.

Have thought about all that was said on Monday last. Your insights were of special note. I am aware of the responsibility you have for the entire "lash-up" of the institution. For you Sir, to take the time and effort to share with those interested in classic films, your knowledge, time, and efforts is a genuine moment in never ending education for all concerned. I am certain all the "seniors" had thought stimulation for the entire evening of 'Red River'. Pity the young people do not realize what they are missing. They can never appreciate the value of "3¢, why that's more silver money than I have seen since the War." Thank you Sir for an enjoyable evening. "Worth driving 20 miles in a snowstorm for." (Groot) Respectfully

O.W. Ervin
(USMC Ret)

21. Mr. O. W. Ervin's thank-you note concerning film, *Red River* – 2004

22. Presentation of certificate by Air Force Colonel Jacqueline Van Ovost (now General Van Ovost) naming Eric as Honorary Commander of the 435th Fighter Training Squadron, Randolph AFB – 2011. General Van Ovost's family operated a banner towing service at North Perry airport in Pembroke Pines, FL – the same airport where Eric began his community college administrative responsibilities at the new South Campus of Broward Community College in 1977.

23. Chicksands 30-Year Reunion in Washington, D. C., mid-1990s:
L to R, Frank Fitzpatrick, Eric, Bill Lawrence

24. Washington, D. C.: Cousin Lee/Pete Reno; Rick Busch; Pat; Gina Reno – 2018

25. Reno siblings – (L to R) Scott, Tim, Judy, Eric and Alan – 2015

26. Eric and Pat: 50th Anniversary – 2018

27. Amanda and Alaina in NYC

28. Patrick and Nancy (in front of "To Kill a Mockingbird")

29. Those who keep us young. Grandchildren. – 2022

Join us for a special dedication & unveiling event celebrating our commitment to art and culture

ALAMO COLLEGES DISTRICT
Northeast Lakeview College

Dr. Veronica Garcia, NLC President, and the Northeast Lakeview College family invite you to a special ceremony recognizing Founding NLC President, Dr. Eric Reno.
Join us for an unveiling ceremony as we name our art gallery the Reno Gallery

Wednesday, April 20, 2022
4pm - 5:30pm
Performing Arts Center Lobby
1201 Kitty Hawk Rd.
Universal City, TX 78148

About Dr. Eric Reno: Dr. Eric Reno served as Founding President of Northeast Lakeview College from 2004-2014. He was a champion of arts and culture for the Northeast side, and an avid moviegoer who launched a community movie series at NLC that included classical movies shown in the college's theater followed by an open discussion. Join us for this special dedication event recognizing Dr. Reno's commitment to culture, student engagement in the arts, and his legacy to education.